# A PIECE OF MY MIND

*by*

# JON STAMFORD

© 2012 JA Stamford. All rights reserved.
ISBN 978-1-291-08908-0

Set in 11 pt Bookman Old Style

# JON STAMFORD

Jon Stamford was educated at Marlborough College and The University of Bath. After some two decades in academic neuroscience, he was diagnosed with Early Onset Parkinson's Disease in 2006. Jon is a full-time writer-scientist and has published three scientific books and three books of humour. He is married with three children.

Dedicated to

my family, who in their own ways, have faced my illness with brutal honesty, exemplary courage and winning humour

# COMMENTS ON PREVIOUS BOOKS 'SLICE OF LIFE' & 'COMING TO TERMS'

In August 2009, Jon Stamford was persuaded to start writing a weekly blog about his and his family's everyday life -- and we should all be grateful. Slice of Life is one year's collection. These are the thoughts, jottings and delightful ramblings of a writer who is not afraid to laugh at himself. I read it at one sitting. That should say it all.

*Review in 'The Parkinson' (Feb 2011)*

I found it very entertaining (I do like the idea of magnetic L plates falling off at 70 mph) and informative (ever since Terry Pratchett mentioned Journey to Samarra in his let's-all-snuff-it lecture I have been wondering what he meant).

*Nancy (London)*

Well I thought A Slice of Life was seriously good, not that I would have expected anything less. I couldn't help thinking of Hunter Davies' Father's Day column in Punch - the antics of various members of his family catalogued each month in a witty and erudite way.

*Claudia (Tunbridge Wells)*

I read (the books) yesterday afternoon and have been raving about them to anyone who would listen since. You accomplish much - science and stories are perfectly intertwined and manage to entertain and inform without being lachrymose. I can't wait for the next installment.

*Emma (Hornsea)*

(It) has had (us) in stitches, especially the one about the sparkly body glitter!

*Zoe (North Carolina)*

My oldest son, my wife, and I sat around our kitchen table tonight while I read your latest. We laughed until we cried.

*Bob (Vancouver)*

Quite brilliant as you are at writing, you have reduced what was a bit of a creative struggle this afternoon to an early evening of tears.....your words have been heartening, provocative and upsetting all at once. I just wanted to say thank you for what you've written.

*Nicola (Tunbridge Wells)*

Love (it). Magnetic ones peel off at 70. Brilliant. Was at a Burns Supper tonight ... with one of my pals who thinks your writing is superb.

*Bryn (Glasgow)*

After having written to tell you how good I found Slice of Life, I have to do it again to tell you that Coming to Terms is just as good

*Trevor (Dortmund)*

# ACKNOWLEDGEMENTS

I would like to thank 'Claire', 'Catherine', 'Alice' and 'Alex', who have generously – if sometimes inadvertently – provided much of the source material for this book.

Without their humour and ability to see the funny side, there would be no book

Claire – for showing me there is sometimes more than one funny side to a joke

Catherine – nobody enjoys slapstick more than you. Remember the windscreen wipers and the scissors...I thought I would wet myself

Alice – simply the funniest person I know when you want to be. LMAO.

Alex – Let's face it, growing up with two big sisters takes a good sense of humour.

# PREFACE

Parkinson's disease, or paralysis agitans as it was first known, is a progressive neurodegenerative condition characterised by tremors, rigidity, slowness of movement and loss of balance.

Every ten minutes of every working day, someone in the UK is diagnosed with Parkinson's, a condition which currently affects more than a hundred thousand UK citizens.

Although Parkinson's is often considered a disease of old age, readers may be surprised to learn that more than one in twenty are diagnosed with the condition before the age of forty.

Despite the nature of the illness, Parkinson's does not kill and symptoms can be ameliorated by drugs, at least in the earlier stages.

Parkinson's is not a death sentence so much as a life sentence.

# NEWLY DIAGNOSED?

It crosses my mind that many of you reading this book may be doing so because you too have been diagnosed with Parkinson's and that you are perhaps looking for guidance or some indication that people can cope, and do cope, with this illness.

I have lived with this now for nearly six years and my best piece of advice to the newly diagnosed would be, in Douglas Adams's words "don't panic". It is possible to live with this condition, and to thrive even. Although Parkinson's will change the things you do, and the way you do them, it will only stop you if you allow it to.

People often react to a diagnosis of Parkinson's in one of two ways. There is the path of destruction, or more accurately self destruction. Don't ask the question "why me?" because it will lead you nowhere. Besides it had to be someone.

Then there is the path of affirmation. Parkinson's will be with you every day and every night. It's an unwelcome houseguest, a squatter even. But until that glorious day when we can evict it from our lives, we would do well to make the best of it.

That's not to say that it's easy. It isn't. It's not say that the path is smooth. Again it isn't. You have Parkinson's, but the Parkinson's does not necessarily have you.

You can be defeated or defined by this condition. Parkinson's can, in so many unexpected ways, give as much as it takes. It's up to you to enjoy those gifts. And you will. Believe me, you will.

# INTRODUCTION

This is becoming a habit. The first book (Slice of Life) about the highs and lows of Young Onset Parkinson's Disease started the ball rolling while the second (Coming to Terms) continued in more or less the same vein. Some of you felt it was a slightly darker book.

On the basis that things seem to go in threes – Father, Son and Holy Ghost – The Good, The Bad and The Ugly – you get the idea – here is the third part of this questionable literary trinity.

I justified the second book on the grounds that large numbers of readers had enjoyed the first, and told me so. The same deal applies here. I like to think of the book lying somewhere in that literary territory between the laugh-out-loud observations of Bill Bryson and the home spun whimsy of Garrison Keillor, albeit imbued with an English accent.

But that's just me. If you enjoyed SLICE OF LIFE and COMING TO TERMS, chances are that this one will float your boat as well.

*Jon Stamford*

October 2012

# OCTOBER

### 4 October 2011 - Bitesize

I have been meaning to do this for a while. I have looked at which pieces have been most popular and why. With internet tools like Google analytics, you can do this sort of thing easily and, to cut a long story short, you want me to cut a long story short. Not for you the lyrical longueurs nor purple prose. No, you want it short and sharp, direct and dirty. And you also want more on Parkinson's. And more of a diary.

So be it.

I have been blogging now for two years and those years have each become the backbone of two books (SLICE OF

LIFE and COMING TO TERMS). This is the third and, in all likelihood, last year of 'Slice of Life' so a change of format is overdue anyway. Shorter, sharper and more Parkie. You've put up with my whimsical weekend meanderings on family life long enough. It's time to turn over a new leaf. Shorter, more personal pieces, more often.

### 5 October 2011 - The nose

It's been one of those days. Our new website is up and running but, for some reason, we are being plagued by frivolous comments from contributors with names like Bobby Cuttlefish. It's a bit galling to read tetchy calls for transparency on the website from someone masquerading as a crustacean. Monkey puzzles indeed.

Just as I'm tiring of sifting through the mailbox for seafood, the phone rings. It is Alex's school with their almost weekly call to tell me that Alex is in sick bay needing collection. If only they operated a loyalty scheme. Usually I find him a whiter shade of pale, head over a bucket, glumly awaiting his ride home. I've stopped taking the Jag.

This time however it's different. He is still in his rugby kit and not short of colour. In fact his face is bright red. Blood red to be specific. And his nose does not appear to be pointing the same direction as the rest of his face.

The town's new hospital has only been open a fortnight and I hadn't planned on availing myself of their services quite this soon. On the face of it the hospital looks impressive. But a two-hour wait to see the triage nurse satisfies me that the building may have changed but the service is still cash-strapped. The hospital also has negligible mobile phone reception, something of a consideration for those who might need to phone relatives for instance.

Just as we are steeling ourselves to the likelihood of missing Top Gear, who should appear from x-ray but Tom, Alex's best friend and up-and-coming legspinner, who has broken his ankle. Freia, his mother, is unamused. This was not how she had planned to spend her birthday.

As darkness falls, we are finally seen by the physician. She confirms that the nose is broken and, in the same breath, tells us that there will be no treatment offered. To Alex, who is expecting to leave casualty looking like the man in the iron mask, this is something of a disappointment.

As we try to leave the hospital, the car park pay point packs up. It is another five minutes before we can get hold of security to let us out. As we wait, all Claire's calls, texts and e-mails arrive at once each more insistent than the last. For about a minute, the phone sounds like a Javanese gamelan.

The painkillers are wearing off for Alex. "How do I look?" He asks.

"Like Mike Tindall" I reply. Alex seems satisfied.

### 6 October 2011 – Meat

A quick early-morning check on the website and all looks good. Bobby Cuttlefish appears to have gone into hibernation for the moment. Claire feeds the puppy and we head off to the station, with her, after a breathless sprint, only just making the 7.20.

A clipped midmorning text message from Claire informs me that as of now she is officially on the Dukan diet, the first five days of which are essentially meat. Nothing more. Just meat. The diet of a Masai lion. I am instructed to bin last night's pasta and clear the decks for the ensuing meatfest.

Clearly some external event has precipitated this decision. Some ill judged comment by a colleague or something similar. I decide not to text back my lukewarm support of this latest dietetic adventure. Besides, I'm on the motorway heading for a lunchtime meeting and in no position to play text tennis.

The meeting goes well. Our opposite numbers seem interested in what we're doing. No tell-tale yawns, twiddling of fingers or doodles on the notepads. They even talk money. And the prospect of more money. We'll see. A two-hour cruise round the M25 later and I'm back home. Alex is comparing sporting injuries with Tom while Alice is loose in Bromley with the fruits of her first pay packet. The work day concludes in a flurry of e-mails and phone calls.

Nine o'clock in the evening and the TV coverage is all of the Tory party conference. Gloom and doom. I need chocolate. And I mean need. And I'm sorry, but chocolate digestives will not do. I need serious chocolate. Dark chocolate, seventy percent cocoa solids at least. Only Tesco is still open. A brief call upstairs to the homework club establishes their specific chocolate needs.

Tesco is empty apart from a handful of shelf stackers and the usual old grubbies trying to buy superstrength lager. I present my purchases at the till. Two bars of Maya Gold, a family pack of Starburst and 500 g of sliced lamb's liver.

"For the dog?" asks Cherie on the till.

"No" I reply "for the wife".

### 7 October 2011 – Music

I have a bit of a soirée planned. My friend Tom, who works for the BBC (or quite possibly doesn't by the end of this week of ill-considered broadcasting butchery), is bringing round some CDs to play. We've planned this for a few weeks. Courtesy of eBay, I've acquired a rather fabulous pair of Quad electrostatic speakers -- about 25 years old but recently reconditioned. And up until now, I've struggled to find an opportunity to play them at anything approaching what I consider to be an appropriate level. Every time they are raised above a whisper, the female contingent of the house insists that I reduce the volume, on pain of immediate emasculation. Tom's presence provides me with a good alibi to don the auditory Lycra so to speak for a bit of a sonic workout.

Aware too that Tom has to drive, I go for alcohol in quality rather than quantity. Rather than pork scratchings and bitter, we opt for toast and foie gras, washed down with a halfway decent Sauternes.

And Tom is, in many respects, the ideal listening partner. Able to spot a serpent, crumhorn or cimbalom at thirty paces, Tom also knows who played what with who and when. His knowledge is encyclopaedic and he turns up clutching an armful of the erudite and eclectic. We listen to CPE Bach, 20th century organ music and a disc by a bizarre bunch of mountain men called Sixteen Horsepower who one suspects would probably eat CPE Bach for breakfast. Literally. They play banjos -- say no more.

I counter with Strauss's Four Last Songs, Joni Mitchell, Brian Eno and a sound effects record of thunder claps, whose principal effect at an earlier dummy run was to send the new puppy scurrying under the dining room table, where it sat whimpering for several minutes until coaxed out with biscuits.

The speakers have a phenomenal level of detail. Not only do you clearly hear the bassoon at the beginning of The Rite of Spring, but also the sound of the key pads opening and closing on the instrument. You can hear the conductor breathing in several places and even, in bar 28, the unmistakable sound of the timpanist breaking wind. It's always the percussionists. Thank goodness I had the subwoofer turned off for that part.

Tom leaves around 11:30 and, as an auditory nightcap, I listen to the Ride of the Valkyries. I swear I can smell napalm.

### 8 October 2011 – Oop North

On paper it seemed a brilliant idea -- to go to Darlington and deliver a talk about new drugs for Parkinson's. At 6 AM on Saturday morning, it seems infinitely less brilliant. A grey rainy day and some six hundred miles of rail travel ahead of me. Still nothing a Madopar capsule, a double espresso and a cinnamon roll can't solve.

I'd forgotten just how dingy King's Cross station is. It's nearly thirty years since I queued on Friday nights for the train to Doncaster. Thirty years of progress, technological advances and leaps forward in customer relations on the railways. Well, everywhere except King's Cross it seems. Apart from the departures board and the new platform 0 (as in zero, how is that possible?), it all seems depressingly familiar. Even down to the constant, irritatingly loud announcements and the drunk from Partick, still unable to find his way home after three decades. If Dante's purgatory has an earthly manifestation, it is King's Cross station.

Darlington is another world, a part of the world I have been away from for too long. Q and I are scheduled to speak in the early afternoon. Veda points out brickwork locomotive sculptures, whilst correcting my lamentably lapsed knowledge of northeastern geography. We arrive just in time to grab sandwiches and big fat chips before Hugh, a fellow shaker, introduces the afternoon session which begins interestingly enough with a bongo drumming class. As occupational therapy for patients, it is near ideal. As a means of clearing one's head before speaking, it falls a little short.

At 2:30, with my ears still ringing after a forty minute drumroll, I launch into my presentation. As usual, I remember starting the talk, with some quip about tough northern audiences, and I remember winding up with a joke about a Gila monster (you needed to be there). The rest is a blur. Then, after a swift journey back to the station in Simon's new Beemer, we are on the train home, a journey much enlivened by an old man's semi-dyskinetic struggle with his dentures. The dentures are winning. At several points in the journey I'm convinced he is going to bite me. Q is struggling to contain the giggles.

Back home at 8:30. Fourteen hours on the road. Shattered. And my sciatica is playing up. I doze on the sofa with a glass of Macallan. It's a cold night. My mind wanders to Partick Jimmy. Will he ever make it home?

### 10 October 2011 – Offal

I can't remember if I mentioned it but we have a new puppy. He is called Louis and is a paper-white standard poodle (Flora, you may remember, died while we were on holiday). We have had him now for three weeks and he has been a big hit with the kids, especially Alex who gave Louis his first exposure to the poodle parlour yesterday, so often a defining moment. For both dog and teenage boy. He – Louis, that is - went in as a grubby country pup with matted hair full of burrs and fox poo. Two hours later he emerged as what I can only describe as a powder puff.

Still these differences are little more than cosmetic. Even if he looks like a giant meringue, he eats like a pig, his ears dragging in his food. He is even messier than me at mealtimes, if such a thing can be imagined. But most revolting of all is his love of tripe.

Now I am proud of my Northern roots and gladly acknowledge my fondness for whippets, James Herriott books, strong tea, Eccles cakes, dry stone walls and rugby league. If I have had enough to drink, I have even been known to laugh at Last of the Summer Wine. And I freely admit a fondness for offal. But, no matter how authentically Northern, tripe is a bridge too far. There is no form of cooking I can imagine that would encourage me to take it from plate to mouth.

But tripe is only part of the problem. Everywhere I look in the fridge there is meat. It could be Christmas. And it can't all be for Louis. The tripe is unquestionably his. But, unless his tastes have been substantially refined by his powder puff experience, the oak-smoked salmon is not. Nor the scallops, I fancy. No, the meatfest is the result of Claire's excursion into the Dukan diet and the shelves are groaning under the weight of dead things. Rather like Claire's metabolism I guess. She's currently at Day 7 of the diet. She is not even allowed chocolate.

I give it a fortnight. Tops.

## 12 October 2011 – Return of The Nose

Wednesday and Alex is due to return to the hospital's ENT clinic for a follow-up appointment following his rugby injury the previous week. He is a little more expansive on the circumstances – he tried to bring down one of the props, was kneed in the face and ended up in a bloody heap at the bottom of a ruck with most of the opposition front row camped on his head. Despite Alex's predilection for hyperbole, his sports teacher corroborates his description of events.

We make a point of arriving in plenty of time. The hospital is poorly served for parking, largely as I understand it, because the council was keen to reduce the carbon footprint. It is one way of reducing waiting lists, I suppose. We circle the car park for twenty minutes, using gallons of fuel, before a space finally becomes available. Hallelujah.

The main atrium is full of bewildered and disorientated faces. In this high tech hospital, you check in, airline style. "This is Alex" I say "he has packed his bag himself and has no liquids on him apart from a can of Fanta" Airline screens direct individual patients to their respective centres of healing. Messages flash up to say "Jenny Walsh to the STD clinic" or "Freddy Packer to Colostomy Services".

But all is not lost. There is a Costa where we find sanctuary before Alex is directed to the unnervingly anonymous "Zone 1". We wait for twenty minutes in Zone 1 before we see the handwritten note to the effect that one should announce one's arrival to reception. Apparently a system advanced enough to direct Alex to Zone 1 is blissfully unaware of his arrival in said zone. A roost of receptionists treats us like aliens for not knowing the system.

Just as I am teeing off for a diatribe about receptionist overstaffing, Alex is called to Consulting Room 9 where a couple of newly qualified doctors quickly pronounce him hale and hearty. Alex is relieved to avoid having his nose rebroken, an outcome several of his school friends had been at pains to tell him would be a cert. He is less pleased to be taken back to school in time for double Geography.

We call security. The car park pay point is still out of action. Alex, full of Fanta, emits a window-rattling burp as the barrier is raised. Adolescents huh

### 14 October 2011 – Tiles

When it comes to interior decoration, Claire and I are poles apart. Which is why, on the whole, we never shop together for any decorative aspect of the family dwelling. We never agree on anything. So shop on your own then, I hear you say.

Even individually it often fails. As for instance on the occasion I brought home a rather attractive sort of pinky red paper lantern lampshade in a sort of Chinese vernacular. It cast a rather fetching and flattering pink glow I thought. Claire raised one disbelieving eyebrow and told me it made the house looked like a Shanghai bordello. Within an hour it had been replaced with a glittery modern chandelier thingy of her choosing, which incidentally took a further two hours of torn fingernails and cursing to unwrap and assemble.

But on Saturday, we were forced to swallow our respective pride and try to pick a mutually agreeable tile design for the bathroom. The builders are due in a couple of weeks and it was only when I checked the small print that I realised it fell to us to provide the tiles.

We started out looking for plain white tiles, floor to ceiling, Claire reasoning that it was simple and looked clean. And she didn't want anything beige. My counter-argument - that it made the bathroom look like a hospital mortuary – whilst not accepted, did at least prompt a rethink. Eventually. To cut a long story short, we picked a glossy, faux marble tile. In beige. Or "cappuccino" as the catalogue called it.

It had taken us the best part of the evening to get this far and we hadn't even touched on the border tiles. We thumbed through the catalogue and agreed on the first halfway decent design.

Neither of us fancied another night on the tiles.


## 15 October 2011 – The Vestry

I've always enjoyed my visits to The Vestry. In the same way that The Priory has become a source of sanctuary for the rich and famous, so has The Vestry become a place of renewal for the footsore Parkie.

A mere stone's throw from The Monument, marking the spot in Pudding Lane where the Great Fire of London started on 2nd September 1666, and within shouting distance of The Old Lady of Threadneedle Street, is The Vestry. Reached by the narrowest of hidden lanes – on a cold winter night it could pass for Nocturnalley – is a small black door. Beside it is an anonymous buzzer. Through the door and straight ahead is the church itself. To the left, behind a heavy bolted door that sticks and creaks in damp weather is The Vestry.

Dimly lit at best, lies a room with five desks of indeterminate vintage, an oak table and a rag-tag handful of office chairs, all at different heights. Tall cupboards with ill-fitting doors bulge with dusty documents. Scurrying quietly among these are occasional church mice or, in summer's still heat, armies of ants.

At the back of the room is a small vestibule with a bathroom on the left and kitchen to the right. The kitchen, where one could not swing a mouse let alone a cat, is damp and cold. Not, you might feel, a place you would seek out. A scary place even. A place to avoid. An unwelcoming place perhaps.

But you would be wrong. Because from these most inauspicious of surroundings runs a global health charity whose bold aim is to put itself out of business by successfully curing Parkinson's disease.

For these individuals finding a cure is more important than finding new office equipment. Every penny spent on a new swivel chair is a penny that cannot be spent on research. Every second spent staring at the city skyline from a swanky office on the 50th floor of a giant office block is a second that could have been spent looking for a cure to Parkinson's. And in the hunt for the cure to Parkinson's, every penny matters and every second counts.

So in this office, a handful of dedicated people ignore the cold, the mice and the damp. Because for them, this is not about egos or prestige. It's not about personal ambition or annual bonuses. It's about one thing, and one thing only. Finding a cure for Parkinson's disease in the shortest time possible. That's all.

And nothing gives me a warmer feeling inside than coming to this dark, damp office. It feels like coming home.

## 19 October 2011 - House and Garden

I tell you, you notice the difference in the weather when you have Parkinson's. A cold snap for anybody else just means another jumper in the daytime or bed socks at night. Not so for me. Cold legs mean muscle-tearing cramps that wake you from the deepest of sleep. And in the daytime, shivers become tremors, and tremors become convulsions. Children point and stare, or hide nervously behind their mothers. Schoolchildren mimic my shuffle. All part of the smorgasbord of indignities this condition seems determined to foist upon me and my fellow Parkies.

Interestingly my dopamine agonist patches seem to work less well in winter too. It's understandable really -- they stick to the skin and gradually leech out drug into my bloodstream. But of course in winter, blood flow to the skin is reduced. Less blood flow equals less absorption of drug surely? I wonder if anyone's looked at this.

We have to be especially careful where we dispose of the used patches too. I've tended to throw them in the bin but, with a new puppy in the house, that isn't an option. Like all puppies, Louis will make off with any identifiable shoe he can find. But Louis also has a penchant for waste paper baskets. To his little canine psyche, the bin is a treasure chest necessitating the vigorous emptying of its contents and their dispersal, as he sees fit, round house and garden. It is not uncommon to find old toothbrushes down by the hen coop.

He does the same for the garden. His current party trick is to bring plants, in their pots, into the living room like prey, shake them wildly in order to kill them and then sit panting attentively for our approval, like some tiny canine Nimrod. I caught him trying to wrestle a small bay tree through the French windows the other day.

It's unclear why he feels the need to blur the boundaries between house and garden but needless to say we are tiring of it. No matter how floral the chintz, sofas are not meant to be covered in potting compost. And finding woodlice in your slippers has not been universally well-received.

Drastic measures are called for. Louis, though he doesn't yet know it, is off to puppy training class tonight. Boot Camp for dogs as I see it.

## 23 October 2011 – Out of Africa

Everywhere I go, I seem to see friends of my children working in improbable locations. Such as the pizza chain named after a popular pub game for instance. Or a fried chicken outlet such as STD or PML or some other three letter acronym. Or even the notable burger chain which I'm reluctant to name. Suffice to say that three hours of McHeartburn was my enduring memory of the last time I ate there.

For the last couple of months, Alice too has been working in a high street retail outlet that sells pots and pans. They all wear matching uniforms like the well drilled culinary army they are. And in the run-up to Christmas, the staff of CakeStand are busier than ever servicing our kitchenware needs. The shelves groan with brandy snaps, liqueur chocolates and rum truffles. In fact anything to which a sprig of miniature holly and the word Christmas can be easily appended to, is a legitimate target.

These Christmas fripperies are, of course, even better in January, when the price for such items plummets to the point where you can indulge your sweet tooth extravagantly and cheaply. They are shedding Christmas staff in January so a few Belgian pralines are neither here nor there. If you are the kind of person who enjoys haggling, and can look them in the eye and keep a straight face, a chocolate bonanza is to be had for mere pennies.

But best of all, Alice told me that when staff leave CakeStand, whether after a few weeks over the Christmas period or after long and glittering retail careers, CakeStand withholds their last pay packet until the uniform has been safely returned. It's a little-known fact that the company collects up all such uniforms and sends them out to the needy in Africa.

It's hard to shake off the notion that somewhere on the plains of the Serengeti, Masai warriors stalk wildebeest or impala, dressed from head to toe as British high street shop assistants.

# NOVEMBER

**2 November 2011 - Trousers trousers trousers**

Last Tuesday was something of a sartorial watershed. I was scheduled to speak at a scientific meeting in the afternoon and was looking for an appropriate form of attire when I had something of a wardrobe failure. Over the last few years I've become a sort of shirt and jeans kind of person. All well and good but there are times when I need to put on my glad rags. Speaking at a scientific meeting is one of those occasions -- suited and booted ideally, or a jacket and trousers as the bare minimum. And therein lay the problem.

No less than eight pairs of trousers available to me but none that I could successfully wear. I would love to report that the trousers are all too big for me as a result of my successful efforts to lose weight since January. But the truth is pretty much the exact opposite. And as button after button ricocheted across the room, it became clear that my options were little more than a pair of brown corduroys. And I'd been using those for gardening.

So, not an auspicious start to the day. And clearly time for action. You may be excused for experiencing a feeling of déjà vu here. Still the time for action was not this morning. Simply finding a way of attending the conference in something other than my pyjamas was a more immediate concern.

Gradually it became clear that my options were either (a) wearing a smart pair of trousers that would almost certainly cut off the circulation to my lower body or (b) turn up at the conference dressed like Bayleaf the Gardener.

Eventually I found I could just, and I mean just, succeed in buttoning up one pair of navy blue trousers without putting fastenings under the kind of forces associated with the gravitational pull of large planets. And as long as I didn't make any sudden movements, there was a least a realistic chance I might be able to breathe as well.

The plan looked almost credible until the Viking decided we were going to La Fromagerie in Marylebone for breakfast. There was clearly no way the dark blue slacks would survive a delicatessen breakfast. Even if I had wanted to, the Viking was not to be thwarted. This was her favourite delicatessen on the planet and I was to share the experience on pain of death.

Two hours, a couple of *pains chocolat* and a cappuccino the size of a basin later, we were at the Royal Society of Medicine, ready for the conference. One of the less obvious advantages of losing your sense of smell is that you are blissfully unaware that you have a definite whiff of potting compost about you. Still my hearing is intact and let me say now there will be dire retribution if I catch the person in the back row whistling The Wurzels' "I've got a brand-new combine harvester".

Oh and La Fromagerie was excellent.

## 6 November 2011- Dublin

I have fond memories of Dublin. A couple of my friends work there and, some years back now, I was interviewed for a very senior academic post. Bittersweet memories to be honest as I was unsuccessful. But there you go.

As luck would have it, I was back in Dublin a few days ago, as a guest of the Parkinson's Association of Ireland and my friend Maggie, talking on Parkinson's Movement. And boy has the place changed.

Take the airport for a start. A colossal glass and steel structure built at the height of the Celtic tiger to accommodate the anticipated hordes of travellers. A triumph of last decade's optimism over today's reality.

Then there are the trams that glide through the city centre. Spanking new yet somehow 'olde worlde' too. But that's the thing with Dublin. The old and traditional sits, cheek by jowl, with the modern in the kind of feisty, garrulous way only the Irish can understand. The Irish treat boom and bust with equal disinterest. This is, after all, the land of Yeats, Beckett and Joyce. Writers who, more than most, celebrated life and death as equals, filling their pages with humanity, with people rather than prices. Life goes on.

And life goes on for the hundred or so Parkies and carers who listened while I walked them metaphorically through the new website. Some asked penetrating questions, some listened attentively, some slept, and some snored. All in all, a typical Parkinson's audience. Our drugs have a lot to answer for. At the end, Maggie and I answered questions on anything and everything. I remember one on alcohol, which I answered with a joke.

An old friend in the military had been given strict instructions by his doctor to give up drinking. I met him one evening after many years and asked him how he was doing. "I haven't had a drink since nineteen fifty eight" he said. "That's tremendous" I said "you must be proud". He looked down at his watch. "Not really" he said "It's only twenty eighteen now".

As Frank Carson would say "It's the way I tell them".

### 11 November 2011 - Poppies

My old school keeps a register of every boy who passed through its gates from 1903 onwards. The register lists the house they were in, when they left the school and, where known, further details such as marriage, career and death.

The school had a strong academic reputation and parents queued up to spend much of their life savings giving their boys the best education they could afford. In January 1907, the register records that thirty six boys joined the school as bright young thirteen-year-olds. Some had brothers. Many were new to boarding school, perhaps waving tearful goodbyes to their mothers and fathers as the school gates closed behind them – much as I did a little over six decades later.

In the summer of 1911, a century ago and now passed into history, those boys left the school as young men, some heading for Oxford and Cambridge, others to Sandhurst where they would train to be officers. Confident young men, schooled to be leaders. Strong flag bearers for the school and their parents' pride and joy.

In less than a decade, the world was a different place. As war tore through Western Europe, the old order was swept away. And a generation and its values with it. Of the thirty six boys who had stood at the school gates a decade earlier, ten were dead, killed in the mechanised slaughter that was the Western front. A lost generation. Three died on the Somme, young officers leading their troops across No Man's Land into a hail of machine gun fire.

For those of us who have never had to fight, their bravery is almost unimaginable, their idealism virtually inconceivable.

And so, at eleven o'clock I stand in silence, this year as every other year. And I will certainly shake. Not because of Parkinson's you understand. But because, through the fog of the generations, I will imagine those ten. Not as the confident young men who fought, but as the anxious boys on their first day at boarding school. And I will think of my own son, the same age as those boys.

Pray God no more wars.

### 15 November 2011 - Sleep

In many respects, it is one of the last frontiers of neuroscience. And one of the more bizarre. We spend nearly a third of our lives asleep and yet, despite the attentions of the finest scientific minds, we still don't really know what sleep is or why we need it. Some argue for a restorative function, or some kind of brain development. Sleep has close relations to memory and may also be an evolutionary protective mechanism. But argue as we might over the merits of each theory, the truth is we know squat about sleep and why we need it. Or even how much of it we need.

The average adolescent for instance, at least on the evidence of this household, needs about sixteen hours a day. And even in those remaining eight hours where they drift fitfully into consciousness, they are unable to perform higher cerebral functions such as conversation. Sixteen hours a day of sleep and eight hours of video games and pizza, punctuated by the occasional grunt is about as much as any of us can hope for as parents. Anyone in the medical profession who wants a definition of 'persistent vegetative state' has only to supply a fifteen year old boy with a couple of DVDs and the TV remote control.

But not everyone needs as much sleep. Or pizza. Margaret Thatcher, or The Spawn of Beelzebub as one of our children's godfathers delights in calling her, famously got by on only five hours a night. As far as she was concerned, sleep was for the weak. And socialists.

Dolphins, you will be impressed to hear, sleep half their brain at a time, alternating every thirty seconds or so. On the evidence of the last lecture I gave, most medical students have also acquired this skill. At no point during the lecture was more than half of the audience actually awake. But I shouldn't be too downhearted -- many of them were still teenagers.

I have developed a new theory about sleep. Over the last few weeks, I've been unable to watch any television in our household because of the female contingent being glued to Strictly Come Dancing, the evening punctuated with oooohhhs from the girls as the dancers strut their stuff, and aarrgghhs from me as Brucie attempts the same. Strangely I have slept like a baby on those evenings.

Nice to see you, to see you z z z z z z z z z z.

## 18 November 2011 – Louis

Louis is bigger now than when I last wrote. Much bigger. And, being male, more assertive. But. despite looking, to all intents and purposes, like a powderpuff with legs, he is a surprisingly engaging beast, always pleased to see us. In fact if anything rather too pleased to see us.

So we are gradually socialising Louis, introducing him to more and more people outside the family. Our theory is that multiple casual visitors will make him less excited than infrequent important visitors in bright colours, bearing gifts. Of course jumping up at guests is really just an expression of friendship. And it is at least a demonstrable improvement on his previously preferred form of greeting, a four paw leap toward the midriff, accompanied by an arbitrary closing of the jaws in the rough area of the genitalia. This does not go down well with guests. On the other hand, as a means of dispersing Jehovah's Witnesses, it can't be faulted.

Puppy class is a help here. Louis is quickly learning a range of commands. He has SIT, STAY and DOWN pretty much button-down now. We're working on FETCH and COME with some progress too. And for the sake of the Jehovah's Witnesses, we should probably add RELEASE as well. Or not.

Of course Louis has his own unique interpretation of a number of these commands. For instance SIT means SIT but only after orbiting the living room and vaulting the sofa. And whilst Louis's response to the word STAY will eventually culminate in a stationary dog, the process will also incorporate a couple of backward somersaults, and a strange kind of four-legged pirouette previously unknown to the World Gymnastic Organisation.

It's no better out in the garden. The command FETCH accompanied by clear pointing to the appropriate item would, you might imagine, be an unambiguous signal. Not so for Louis for whom the command means run hysterically around the garden for several seconds, bark at the chickens, chase the neighbour's cat over the fence and then pick up the nearest available stick and amble towards you. Always assuming that you haven't lost interest by this stage and long since vanished indoors for a cup of tea. Still he's only a puppy.

And we haven't seen a Jehovah's Witness in weeks.

## 22 November 2011 - The Talking Plate

A company in Sweden has invented a talking plate. No, really. I'm not making this up. And why, I hear you ask, would anyone want such a thing? Perhaps it's aimed at the lonely or single.

"Hello dear" it might say "and how was your day?" Or it might regale you with the evening news or the latest gossip from Mrs Truscott at number thirty seven. The possibilities are endless.

Endless certainly, but in this case hardly explored. Because the plate in question is not the erudite interlocutor one might hope for, constantly engaging your banter with quips and repartee, whilst offering a position on the world banking crisis or today's episode of The Archers. No sirree -- expect no propositions from Wittgenstein here. All the plate will do is tell you to eat your food more slowly. That's it. Nothing else. Except nag. Many may feel they have that base covered already.

No matter how isolated your existence, the stupid thing will still nag you. You may be so overweight and your self-esteem at rock bottom that it will only take one more thing to tip you over the edge. Then along comes the cheerily blunt Talking Plate, tableware's answer to Dr Kevorkian, to tell you that you are a pig. Short of handing you a revolver, it's hard to see how the plate could be any more helpful in bridging the gap between you and your maker.

I can't help feeling that these plates would be much better suited to a Swiss assisted suicide clinic than a domestic dining table.

The manufacturers I understand produce the plate in many languages. But is that enough I ask. What Glaswegian is ever going to listen to a plate telling him, in perfect Etonian vowels, to go easy on the deep fried Mars bars? In any case, you would need to have different Talking Plates for different circumstances and social strata. There might be the Brookside plate "Ceealm down, ceealm down ya fat b*****d" for some, or the Gosford Park plate "I say old chap, jolly poor show" for those with stiff upper lips.

I could see a market for a more positive, life enhancing sort of plate though. An Assiette Bon Viveur maybe. It would sound rather like Brigitte Bardot.

"Pssst, Jon" it would whisper "zer ees a leetle Roquefort and Sauternes een ze freedge..."

"No, ma petite assiette, I am trying to be good"

"Maybeee some foie gras on toast zen?"

"Oh go on then"

Or there might be a Yorkshire version

"Ee get this down thee. Tha's nowt but skin and bone"

"Honestly, Plate, I can't eat another thing. Besides I weigh thirteen stone"

"Nay lad, tha's lean as a whippet. Have some more of my mam's Eccles cakes. She made 'em special wi that Aorta suet"

"Atora surely?"

"If tha says so"

Either way I don't see talking plates taking off. But then I said that about the iPad.

### 29 November 2011 – 544

Five hundred and forty four turns out to be the exact number of sweets in a jar at Alex's school fair. For twenty pence, the kids were invited to guess the number of sweets with the person guessing correctly winning the jar itself. The lucky winner, who presumably also now qualifies for cut rate dental work, was none other than Alex himself.

In case you wonder what kind of vessel could hold this many sweets, let me just say that it is about the size of a large watermelon. And weighs about the same. And in case you further wonder how long five hundred and forty four sweets would last the average fourteen-year-old boy, the answer is nowhere near as long as you might think.

This cornucopia of candy contains sugary things, fizzy things, chocolatey things, minty things and lots of lollipoppy things. "Er, those would-be lollipops Dad" says Alex. It even contains some false teeth made out of something similar to wine gums. Which is ironic really, because if Alex eats the whole lot, he will be in need of the real thing (philosophical point -- can there be such a thing as real false teeth?).

As far as I can tell, the cheap end of the sweet market seems to have been cornered by Haribo, a German company founded in 1920 -- hardly you would have thought a time when Germans had money to spend on such frivolities. Still, a company that survives under such economic austerity is clearly well placed for world domination. And so it seems to be.

In this country, we can't seem to produce sweets any more and, taking a leaf out of BMW's book, Haribo has evidently put paid to the British sweet industry in much the same way BMW despatched Austin Rover. Most of the sweets of my childhood seem confined to the pages of history -- Liquorice allsorts, Everton mints, chocolate limes, blackjacks, gobstoppers, pear drops, strawberry bonbons, humbugs, wine gums, jazzies, Parma violets, dip dabs, and love hearts.

And what of sherbet fountains? When I was ten, they were my idea of heaven. Tingly, sharp and sweet. And they made you sneeze. But you could never share one, especially with a girl. Because to share a sherbet fountain with a girl was, as any ten year old boy would tell you, tantamount to a proposal of marriage. Ah happy days!

# DECEMBER

**10 December 2011 - Chunder**

It's been a busy few days to say the least. In the space of exactly forty eight hours I have been interviewed on camera in Stansted for a corporate training video about how to better understand people with Parkinson's, attended an all day management brainstorming session in Brussels, and lectured to graduate entry medical students about Parkinson's in the Midlands. My forty eight hours breaks down into just over nine hours speaking, twelve hours driving, three hours flying, five hours waiting for weather-delayed flights, nine hours sleeping, four hours of working lunches or dinners, two hours writing blogs, two hours answering e-mails, an hour in the shower and half an hour beating my personal best on Angry Birds. (Fruit Ninja wouldn't load). Oh, and thirty minutes well spent in the Neuhaus chocolate factory in Brussels, speedsampling pralines.

If it weren't for all the business cards I picked up along the way, I wouldn't have the slightest idea who I had been speaking to, when or where. Drive-talk-drive-fly-drive-sleep-eat-talk-scribble-drive-fly etc etc. When I haven't been deafened by jet engines, it has been the soft purr of the Jag to keep me company. The number of empty coffee cups in the Jag confirm that this is not a life pattern consistent with longevity.

So by the time I arrived home, dazed and confused, just after lunch today, I half expected that the family had all but forgotten what I looked like. As I pulled up on the drive, Claire returned in the other car with Alice. Their behaviour seemed to confirm my worst fears. Neither spoke to me but headed straight indoors. Just as I was about to reprimand both for their flagrant disregard for my feelings, the sound of my younger daughter vomiting explained all.

Food poisoning was her considered diagnosis, between bouts of retching. Casting her mind back over things recently eaten, my money is on the calamari at a local Italian restaurant. I gave up any further efforts to establish causality. It's hard to have a proper conversation with someone who has their head over a toilet. Still, she perked up considerably when I said she could probably sue the restaurant.

Taken ill this morning whilst at work, she had only narrowly avoided pebbledashing a customer in Cakestand. Strangely, the staff manual, which details every conceivable facet of good customer relations, is reticent on the matter. "Do not eat in front of customers. Do not swear in front of customers. Do not push or jostle customers. Do not raise your voice with customers".

But in amongst this litany of good advice, there is not a single line to indicate that you are not permitted to throw up over them. Think on that next time you have the shop assistants scouring the stockroom for last year's novelty corn forks.

I think a corporate training video is in order.

## 12 December 2011 –
## Things That Go Bump in the Night

Or more accurately go *scrape, twang, crash, tinkle, glug glug glug*. Whatever the sound, it still achieves the same result -- you are instantly half conscious, wondering what you have been dreaming about. Only when the wife says "did you hear that?" are you suddenly wide-awake. We listen for a moment for further sounds whilst trying to work out what might have caused what we both heard. Claire yawns, concludes, with breathtaking *sang froid*, that it is "probably nothing" and, within seconds, is fast asleep again. On the other hand, I am now bolt upright in bed, aware of my heart thumping, and inevitably quivering like a jelly. Torn between a warm bed on a chilly night and investigating said sound, Claire and I have reached entirely different conclusions. While Claire heard nothing more than perhaps a mouse losing its footing, my imagination has conjured a gang of armed robbers pilfering my drinks cabinet before murdering us all in our beds.

Clearly, as head of the household (or as near as any male gets to be with three females in the house), it falls to me to investigate. The soft breathing sounds coming from the other side of the bed confirm that this will be a solo investigation. Pausing only to pull on my Y-fronts and unsheath a 19th century cavalry sabre I keep under the bed, I tiptoe down stairs. In my mind, I am Harry Flashman. In reality, it's Homer Simpson. But since I know which stairs creak and which do not, the element of surprise is on my side.

I silently open the living room door. Nothing. The music room. Nothing. The conservatory. Nothing. The kitchen. Nothing. Clearly the sight of a potbellied middle-aged Parky in his underwear brandishing an oversized steak knife has seen the scoundrels on their way. Satisfied that my swift actions have averted a massacre, I return to my (by now cold) bed. Strangely I fall asleep.

Two hours later the alarm clock goes off. When I open the shower door, the cause of the night's tomfoolery becomes apparent. The shower basket, attached by suction pads to the wall, wasn't any more and its contents were distributed over the floor of the shower. It all made sense – *scrape (the basket sliding down the wall), twang (the last suction cup popping), crash (the basket hitting the floor), tinkle (the aftershave bottle shattering), glug glug glug (said expensive aftershave vanishing down the plug hole).*

Still, in the middle of the night, almost no explanation makes sense.

## 15 December 2011 – Stilts and caterpillars

One of the great joys of having fashion-conscious teenage daughters is the almost endless supply of material for this blog. Last night is a case in point. Around eight o'clock I sit down to put down a few of my usual meanderings and find myself staring at a blank page. And that's unusual for me because normally I can rant on demand. And it's not unknown for me to be grumpy. But to be bereft of ideas is unusual. While I wait for inspiration's muse, I start on a shopping list.

I try everything. Word salad, free association, reading the local newspaper. Even -- God help us -- poetry. After a few minutes of pointless chewing on the end of a strange tasting ballpoint pen, I am about to give up when Alice calls from her bedroom for an opinion on her choice of attire for the sixth form party that night.

It is a pretty desperate scenario for any teenage girl to have to ask their father for fashion advice. Nonetheless, I agree to do so. I dutifully close my eyes.

"What do you think?" says Alice.

I open my eyes and am immediately lost for words. Firstly, my daughter is a good six inches taller than she was an hour ago. Only when I look down at her feet, drawn by a vivid nail varnish does it become apparent that this is attributable less to a record-breaking growth spurt than the fact that she is wearing the tallest pair of stilettos I have ever seen. The kind of shoes that settle arguments at Sicilian weddings. And more to the point, the kind of shoes that lead to spinal injuries in the wearer.

And it doesn't end there. Despite the fact that the temperature is dropping below zero outside, younger daughter appears to believe that the party venue will be a tropical island. That is the only rational explanation for the kind of flimsy, glittery gold dress thing she is wearing. I am lost for words I have handkerchiefs with more material in them.

She will not tell me the price so I can only assume that it was preposterous. Factoring in the size and weight of the garment, a bit of mental arithmetic leads me to the conclusion that it costs about as much as bullion.

But the pièce de résistance, only apparent when Alice turns round to face me are the false eyelashes. I bite my tongue till I can taste blood to avoid laughing aloud. I have seen pictures of rare South American caterpillars less extravagantly hairy than these. Each eyelash affords a magnificent canopy to the eyes that I assume still reside beneath.

And there you have it. In the space of ten seconds, enough material for the blog. And suddenly I remember why the biro tasted funny. I add cotton earbuds to the shopping list.


## 17 December 2011 - Newsletter

Each year this time, those unfortunate enough to be on our Christmas card list live in dread of the arrival of this year's Christmas missive from the Stamford family. Now I don't know for a fact but I still have a gut feeling that many of these newsletters find their way into the dustbin without being read. And in a way I can kind of see their point. These things are almost impossible to write right. Because unlike a personalised epistle, these newsletters go identically to the wealthy and poor, the healthy and ailing, and to close friends (who only saw you last week and know this already) and distant acquaintances who, unless you list all your children's names, will not have the slightest idea which of the fifteen Jons they know actually has Parkinson's. This can lead to misunderstandings.

Inevitably you have to make certain assumptions of familiarity -- you shouldn't need to say for instance "Alice (that's my middle child)" enjoys horseriding or "Claire (my wife of twenty some years) has a new car and vows never to buy a diesel again". But equally you should not assume that everyone knows that Catherine's boyfriend is "gradually falling under the spell of Wagner". Which he is -- even if he doesn't know it yet.

So what is the cut-off for newsworthiness? The death of a pet such as a guinea pig is probably not front-page news. The demise of a pet piranha or chameleon probably is. Especially if they have a ridiculously inappropriate name like Schnuckum. A family member having a triple valve cardiac bypass is almost certainly newsworthy. A radical haemorrhoidectomy, no matter how much suffering was involved, clearly isn't.

And the tone of the newsletter is critical. On the one hand you want to impart all the news about the children in an upbeat manner. But it is equally imperative not to seem smug or complacent. Sentences like "Prunella had a great gap year at CERN, and found something called the Higgs Boson. We are all jolly proud" never go down well with recipients whose son has just been excluded for the third time this year for punching his physics teacher. Being needlessly light on detail is equally taboo. "Tristan had to miss Clarissa's group 3 flute exam because he was stuck in Stockholm" is clearly a misrepresentation when it transpires that Tristan was collecting the Nobel prize for medicine. And the recipients have been waiting for opportunity to congratulate him.

The same rules hold for holidays. If you've been in Venice for a fortnight at the Gritti, and most of your readers had to scratch around for a week in Bognor, expect fewer Christmas cards next year. And don't even dream about mentioning work-related, expenses-paid trips to the Maldives, Bahamas or Seychelles. It's for your own safety. Believe me.

Anyway, fortunately none of the above applies to us. Once again I'm forced to pad out the letter with family trivia. Nobody discovered a fundamental particle and Alex's 4th XI Player of the Year is as close as we've got to any serious silverware.

So this year again, the newsletters plop into letterboxes.

"A newsletter from Jon and his family"

"Jon?"

"You know -- lives in Kent"

"Oh, thank goodness. I thought it was that bore with Parkinson's for a minute".


### 19 December 2011 – Strictly no more.

For the watching millions, the drama is captivating, the tension unbearable. But, as Europe burns, well the Euro at least, the gaze of half the Stamford household is on Blackpool and the final of Strictly Come Dancing. Elsewhere in Europe, wall-to-wall media bulletins cover the moribund state of the Euro. Chancellor Meerkat and President Sarcastic announce yet another comically implausible salvage package. Meanwhile in Blackpool, the music rises and the dancers glide onto the stage in layers of mascara and showers of sequins. And it's not just the boys -- the girls have dressed up too.

The Stamford television is 'booked' for the evening. Financial oblivion, civil unrest, and the rise of nationalism are mere pimples on the horizon compared with the immediately pressing question of whether Jason, Chelsea or Harry will be crowned the best "Person Who Is Famous for Something Else but It Turns out They Can Dance a Bit As Well". I'm sure the trophy expresses it more pithily but that's the gist of it.

I'm not letting any cats out of the bag if I reveal that the winner was Harry. That's the Harry who is a professional drummer and presumably knows a thing or two about rhythm. This should come as no surprise surely? Predictably, the series ends in tears of disappointment and joy. All human drama is here -- there are winners and losers until one of the inevitable avalanche of platitudes makes it clear that they are all winners -- in stark contrast to the unfolding European drama where it appears we are all losers. At least in both cases, it amounts to the same thing -- a prolonged multinational blub.

So, moving on, how are we to spend our Saturday evenings now that this tearful, glitterball polkafest is over?

Well we could always tune into the Merkel and Sarkozy Euro show. Full of sharp moves and, unlike Strictly Come Dancing, this show will run and run....

## 22 December 2011 – Cocktails

The pre-Christmas run up follows a familiar pattern. Around the end of November, a brief review of the drinks cabinet reveals a few ethanolic shortcomings. And the wine cellar is no better. There are gaping holes which necessitate, at the very least, a major excursion to Oddbins or Majestic for burgundy by the bathful, hogsheads of port, buckets of Beaujolais. Not to mention those insanely strong liqueurs made by every Catholic monastic order known. Franciscans, Benedictines, Cistercians -- they all seem determined to outbid each other in some sort of distillery drag race.

But not this year. In a time of economic hardship, not least for ourselves it has to be said, it seems vaguely obscene to be purchasing even more alcohol. So this year I have decided to buy nothing. That's right -- not a single bottle of beer. Nichts. Nada. Visitors to our house will not be offered bitters from several counties, lagers from half the EEC, nor wine from every weingut, chateau or bodega in the Western Hemisphere. No, those days are over.

This year, we drink from what we have.

I mean it.

This newfound attitude has brought a more critical examination of the contents of the drinks cabinet. A couple of days ago I pulled out every single bottle and triaged them into three categories -- things I would probably never choose to drink even if I lived to be a hundred, things I could imagine myself drinking at some point, and things I had a fair intention of drinking that same evening.

Into the "pour it down the sink before the kids drink it" category fell a number of dusty bottles from the darkest recesses, from which the labels had detached or faded over the many intervening years. In some cases, the caps were rusted or the contents had partially evaporated. Some, I'm pretty sure, were only intended for cleaning wounds. Or embalming. It's not every day you come across a bottle of absinthe either.

Into the "hand me a glass" cohort fell a couple of malt whiskies, inexplicable survivors from my birthday a couple of months ago, an '85 Graham's port and a bottle of Tokay with more puttonyos than you could shake a stick at.

The "well maybe if I was thirsty" group was the largest, perhaps a reflection of that indecision that seems to plague all Parkies. But, irrespective of the size of the group, this is the fertile breeding ground for future cocktails. In this category, drinks like ginger wine, blue Curaçao, Drambuie and Kahlua find their spiritual home (boom boom).

So, throughout December, I've been experimenting and creating cocktails previously unknown to man. Or at the very least unnamed. And in many cases, deservedly so. For some, so bereft of ideas have I been that I have even named the day's creations by jabbing my finger arbitrarily into the newspaper for suitable juxtapositions. This accounts for the 'Miliband Boson' for instance. And I apologise. Well, sort of.

So if you drop round to our house expecting a chilled glass of Chablis or a drop of claret, you may be in for a disappointment. But if you're in the mood for alcohol adventure, then you're probably ready for your first 'Exploding Halibut'. Shall I make that a double?

### 24 December 2011 – Sorted!

It's official -- Christmas is under control. No more work until the middle of next week. Even the tone deaf ten-year-old ruffians masquerading as carol singers have given up on us. Amazing after Claire had given them five pounds the first time they knocked. This kind of unprovoked generosity usually ends with all the urchins in a five mile radius descending on the house like locusts. Don't get me wrong -- I like music as much as the next man but five pounds for a single growled verse of "We Wish You a Merry Christmas" is a certifiable act of lunacy. Five pounds! You could have had the Vienna Boys Choir for that money. What was she thinking? Three vocally challenged hoodies do not, in my view, qualify for the kind of donations associated with the relief of famine in Africa.

Just as I start ranting, Alex appears, makes a gesture to me to zip it and encourages me to deep breathe. "In the zone Dad. Now".

Anyway, back to the point. Christmas is sorted. Claire has taken care of all shopping. And I mean all. Every last bit. From the mince pie for Santa to the pickled walnuts that are my special foible. What a saint.

All that remains for me to do before tomorrow is to get Claire her present. Freia is confident she knows exactly what Claire wants for Christmas. And how does she know? This information it transpires has emerged from the convivial needlework and conversation group that both attend on Tuesday evenings. These 'stitch and bitch' sessions (their words not mine) flit from subject to subject like butterflies -- until the wine really flows, when the focus shifts to the many perceived advantages of quality woollens over the average male of the species.

Not surprisingly, I decide that information obtained under such circumstances is unlikely to be a reliable indicator. In any case, after considerable reflection and deliberation, I have chosen a Christmas present. I think it's safe to say that it is an electrical product which contributes to enduring marital harmony more than anything else you could imagine.

I'm talking of course of a satnav. Why, what were you thinking?

## 27 December 2011 – Red for danger

Only when you reach Christmas morning, do you realise quite how ill-prepared you are. There are toys to be unwrapped, things to be screwed together, and batteries to be inserted. If you're unlucky, you will need glue and the power to placate small children while it dries. And if you're really unlucky, you will have to read the instructions. Suffice to say that there is no greater humiliation for a man.

It therefore makes sense to have a screwdriver to hand. Some sixty people each year are admitted to hospital with injuries sustained using sharp knives instead of screwdrivers. Why would you use a knife anyway when you can always resort to the Birmingham screwdriver, better known in the rest of the world as a hammer. Let's face it -- you wouldn't try to cut bread with a screwdriver so why would you use a bread knife to put your son's Scalextric together? In 2006, five people were admitted to hospital with injuries sustained as a result of out-of-control Scalextric cars. It is as bad as the M25 on a Friday night.

In fact, Christmas is fraught with danger. Statistics show that four people every year will kill themselves by testing 9V batteries using their tongue. Yes, you were that close.

The combination of alcohol, mains electricity and a room temperature IQ is a formula for trouble but it takes a special breed of idiot to water a Christmas tree while the fairy lights are connected. Still, three people every year meet their maker doing just that. Incredibly, a similar number eliminate themselves from the gene pool each year munching their way though glass baubles in the tragically mistaken belief they were made of chocolate. Parkinson's has robbed me of much of my sense of taste and smell but I would like to believe that I have sufficient residual sensory apparatus to still tell the difference between chocolate and glass.

Inevitably, alcohol plays a part in most festive injuries. Each Christmas, four people break arms pulling crackers or trying to wrestle the TV remote off their siblings, to say nothing of the five hundred people each year who clog up

A&E with injuries induced by ill-advised attempts to open beer bottles with their teeth. They are probably among the eight each year who fracture their skulls on the toilet bowl while being sick. Classy.

But, as a father of once small children, my heart goes out to the hundred people since 2000 who have pieces of plastic toys surgically extracted from the soles of their bare feet, each Christmas.

Bet they don't complain about getting slippers next year.

## 29 December 2011 – Monopoly

I remember quite clearly how it began. Alex says "Nothing like a nice family game of Monopoly" and, with varying degrees of assent, the family agrees. Some even ask why we don't play more often.

I say nothing.

I should probably declare immediately that the Stamfords have a disquietingly competitive nature when it comes to board games. Stamfords play to win. Even in Monopoly. If you can imagine the Borgias playing Monopoly, you would not be far wrong.

For this reason, I tend not to play board games. Even my mother, meek as a mouse in most things, turned to the dark side when it came to games, even being known to upend the board when things turned against her. Whatever gene it is that makes the Stamfords so competitive also makes them very poor losers. I can also say with the confidence of a biological scientist, that the gene is autosomal dominant.

Everyone in the family has their own philosophy on how to win the game. Alice likes the red and orange properties, while Alex is determined to own the ultraexpensive streets clustering immediately before Go. My approach has always been to quietly buy the stations, thereby conducting a silent war of attrition. £50 here, £100 there, gnawing quietly at the purse. More recently my approach has been rumbled to the extent that none of the family will ever sell me a station except under extreme duress.

To create further friction, there are of course a number of minor ambiguities in the rules and local customs that can make for significant misunderstandings. For instance, when I grew up "Free Parking" was nothing other than a neutral corner -- it neither rewarded you with wads of cash nor sent you to prison. Claire grew up with a different rule -- that all fines, speeding tickets, house repair fees and so on were paid into a central fund and whoever landed on the aforementioned square, received whatever was in the pot. This is all very well when the pot is a mere £50 but sparks a civil war when, as it does tonight, the pot exceeds £3000. In an instant, what started as an episode of Little House on the Prairie suddenly becomes a cross between an Agatha Christie murder mystery and Lord of the Flies.

First to leave the game is Catherine, after overstretching herself buying properties like scratchcards. Having just written her a very real cheque for next term at college, this laissez-faire attitude rather drains the colour from my cheeks. Next out of the Big Brother household as it seems to be fast becoming, is Alex. With the battleship as his token, he falls to the classic double whammy, landing first on Claire's Park Lane packed with houses and forcing him to mortgage everything he owns. His next throw – double 1, takes him to Mayfair, resplendent with a large red hotel. Already holed below the waterline, this quickly scuttles his battleship and, since the Monopoly game was his idea, also his evening. Bad enough in its own right but probably further exacerbated by a loud "Mwah ha ha" from his sister -- a reaction curtailed only by the immediate community chest directing her to pay the repairs on some 20 houses and hotels.

My station strategy is also fatally flawed, having only been able to secure three of the four. Without Liverpool Street, the remaining three cannot fully realise their mid-term revenue targets -- you see what I mean, I'm even beginning to speak like these people. Aaaaargh.

I limp on for another half an hour, winning a crossword competition and receiving second prize in a beauty contest, the first greeted with cries of "nerd", the second with rather too spontaneous derisive laughter. It is not even worth trying to sell my Get Out Of Jail Free card to those family members still incarcerated. At this point in the game, prison is the only safe place. Everyone would rather do their porridge than run the gauntlet outside. Inevitably it is not long before an unfortunate Chance advances me to a hotel-infested Pall Mall and financial oblivion.

Alex's words echo in my ears "nothing like a nice family game of Monopoly". He's right -- this is nothing like one.

# JANUARY

**1 January 2012 – Quiz**

We more or less tossed a coin. Freia and Anton lost so we went round to their gaff for New Year. 'We' in this case meant Claire, Alex and myself. Catherine had left mid-afternoon for her boyfriend's place in Surrey and Alice had headed out to a friend's 18th, clutching a luminous green bottle of Apple Sours. But only after applying a second layer of fake tan – the first coat didn't take. Alex, ever helpful younger brother, said she had overdone it to the extent that she looked Portuguese. This impudence earned him a single raised eyebrow that said "One more misplaced quip at my expense and I will fillet you with a steak knife, don't think I won't".

And that wasn't the only crisis. Somehow I have mislaid a case of champagne, surplus from the September party. I know it's in the house somewhere but can't quite place it and, like most Parkies, am obsessive enough that I will have to find it. It will bother me. Because I want to make champagne cocktails.

There are many different ways of making a champagne cocktail but ours involves a sugar cube, a shot of brandy and then the rest of a glass of champagne. And very good it is too.

But the days when I could drink all evening are long since gone. Two glasses and a backlog of sleep loss meant that I was snoring by nine o'clock. While the adults quaffed champagne, the kids entertained themselves with the contents of a gigantic cracker Claire had found in a shop in town. I'm not sure that the tinsel wig I wore was quite such a good idea with hindsight. I look like a member of Spinal Tap.

Fortunately I had the antidote – a quiz to while away time until midnight. Freia, having read the previous column, was wisely steering clear of any mention of Monopoly for fear that things might kick off like the 1981 Toxteth riots. Having recently redecorated, a state of 'managed decline' was probably not uppermost in her mind.

Still, a quiz is not without its risks. The two families divided into three teams and it was clear who knew their stuff and who didn't. Fifty questions sorted the wheat from the chaff. The winners, Claire and Freia, achieved a score of twenty two which, though creditable, revealed a lamentable lack of religious knowledge for two practising Catholics. What famous catholic tribunal started in 1223? The Inquisition. I had expected them to walk that one.

Let me clear up some other misunderstandings while I'm here. The famous quotation *The female of the species is more deadly than the male* is by Rudyard Kipling and not Lady Gaga. For that matter, when asking for the name of the pianist husband of Jacqueline Du Pre, the name I was looking for was Daniel Barenboim and not 'Mr Du Pre'. The lines *A horse, a horse, my kingdom for a horse* is classically attributed to Richard III. Not Lester Piggott. And finally, banon, mimolette, Monterey Jack and samsoe are all types of cheese. Not slang terms for gonorrhoea.

As Big Ben rang in the New Year, we stood outside in some decidedly unnecessary drizzle while Tom attempted to light the fireworks Anton had assembled for our entertainment. No faffing about with tapers and a parade of rockets or Roman candles -- these were three self-contained units with a range of fireworks all lit by a single fuse. Each was the size of a basketball and looked like a depth charge or a Second World War Russian rocket battery.

For the average fireworkhead, you can't beat the smell of cordite. After five minutes of cracks, bangs, thumps and banshee shrieks, it was all over. But for a moment there, we could have been in Toxteth.

## 2 January 2012 – Choppers and planes

Unquestionably the best Christmas present received by any member of the family, well in my view at least, was the remote control helicopter. Approximately fourteen inches (no idea what that is in modern units) in length, it is Alex's pride and joy. And I can see why. For approximately an hour of charge, the helicopter provides twelve minutes of flight. That seems pretty impressive to me. And if I'm honest, I would probably trade my (admittedly rather fine) blue jumper for it.

The packaging confidently assures the reader that the helicopter is suitable for both indoor and outdoor flying. Outdoor certainly -- it takes off and flies in reasonably confident circles with a bit of practice and can even be landed without catastrophic damage. Indoors it is a very different proposition. Although the stiller air makes flying easier, this advantage is largely negated in the confined spaces indoors.

Despite being made of plastic and therefore considered safe by the manufacturers, the high rotor speeds lend the device a considerably more dangerous air. Coming into contact with the mantelpiece for instance does more than knock a few Christmas cards onto the floor. And therefore the prospect of rotor blades scything their way through bone china ornaments and other heirlooms makes the living room a No-Fly Zone.

But despite these, in Alex's view, Draconian flying restrictions, the chopper has rather rekindled his interest in aircraft, dormant for many years. So much so that he suggested last week, and I took minimal persuasion, that we should go to the Imperial War Museum's aeronautical branch at Duxford.

The museum was full of pretty much every British aeroplane I had ever assembled from an Airfix kit. Shackleton, Lancaster, Sunderland, Mosquito, Beaufighter, and Anson. It was like my childhood in 1:1 rather than 1:72 scale. I could have stayed there forever but, as Alex reminded me, there were four further hangers to visit.

In a brief gap in the weather -- did I forget to say that it was a mix of horizontal rain and hail -- we headed for the American air force hangar, following a group of Hassidic Jews with Tourette's (really), surely one of the more bizarre coach parties at Duxford that day. Alex and I had the hangar more or less to ourselves, the echo of our footsteps punctuated only by the occasional bleep and squawk from the Hassidim, clustered around a B-17. In front of a Stratofortress was a small snack bar where we stopped for a sandwich and a glass of Dandelion and Burdock while the Hassidim shrieked and whooped their way through the Gulf War display.

I don't think I've ever seen such a tightly packed collection of every American aircraft of significance since the First World War. From the Spad to the U2, the Flying Fortress, Superfortress and Stratofortress, A-10, Liberator, and goodness knows what else, this was a jawdropping display of military Americana. But nothing impressed me more than the Lockheed SR 71 Blackbird. It's hard to imagine a craft that looked more menacing than this brooding epitome of darkness. Highlight of the day for me.

But strangely not for Alex. Watching his eyes widen at each new aircraft, he reserved the bulk of his superlatives for a single aeroplane. Which one I hear you ask? Perhaps the McDonnell Douglas Phantom's speed and destructive capability? Maybe the dart-like perfection of Concorde, still surely the most beautiful aeroplane ever to take to the air? Or how about the English Electric Lightning, that definitive Cold War interceptor?

None of the above as it turns out. The aeroplane that captured Alex's imagination more than any other was the Vulcan bomber. And I can see what he means. I grew up in South Yorkshire not far from what is now Robin Hood International Airport. But in the 1960s, this was RAF Finningley. And Finningley was home to a Vulcan squadron.

Each year my father and I would go to the annual Finningley air show. And these were the days not of small-scale biplanes and helicopter display teams that seem to be the currency of modern air displays. No sirree. Air displays in the 1960s meant fast low-level flyovers by supersonic interceptors and huge bombers that darkened the sky. Thrilling stuff for the average ten-year-old boy, treated to an endless parade of the latest military hardware.

But nothing epitomised the pride of the RAF more than the air show finale. In the kind of display unthinkable in these cost-, health- and safety- cosseted days, the Finningley airshow ended with a six Vulcan scramble. And if you were down the far end of the runway, as we often were, the sight of half a dozen delta wing V bombers gathering speed in succession was riveting. The sound quite literally took your breath away. If hell has a soundtrack, this would be it.

The Vulcan bomber. Good call Alex.

## 6 January 2012 -- Bedtime reading

Even at my most somnolent, I'm not the kind of person who goes to bed at ten o'clock on the dot, neatly brushing my hair and teeth, buttoning up my pyjamas to the top and carefully placing my slippers neatly under the bed. No sirree. I am more likely to doze off in front of a late-night movie or test match coverage from Australia, glass of whisky in hand, snoring myself awake at one o'clock in the morning and staggering dishevelled to bed.

On the occasions that I do go to bed at a reasonable hour, I still find myself unable to sleep until I have let my brain wind down. A few games of solitaire on the iPad perhaps, a stab at the Telegraph crossword or, more recently, dipping into some of my old books.

I am one of those people who are destined to receive books, booze, aftershave or jumpers at Christmas. On the assumption you get what you need, that makes me an illiterate, tatty, smelly alcoholic. Well thanks guys.

So when in doubt give Jon a bottle of Talisker, a Fair Isle jumper or an Armani spray. Although, being evidently an alcoholic, he'll probably drink it anyway. Or play safe and buy him a book.

I'd like to read more. I'm not a particularly cerebral reader and I will at least pick up most books. Except Jeffrey Archer. Mostly I find I read factual books these days and, as my eyesight has deteriorated, books with pictures. I hardly ever read novels now. Increasing impatience puts paid to that. I like to dip into books too and the novel format does not lend itself to that treatment. Besides, most bore the pants off me. By the time I have finally written a novel off as terminally dull, several chapters may have elapsed. And with Parkinson's, that sort of floundering time investment merely annoys me.

So my bedside table is an eclectic mixture of books on various subjects. Things I know I will like. There is "*Science and Religion*" by Thomas Dixon. It calls itself a very short introduction and although only 140 pages, is written in such a vanishingly small font or as to be almost illegible. The magnifying glass necessary to read the text is bigger than the book itself. I'm currently rumbling through the chapter on mind and morality. Chewy.

A relaxing and crispy antidote is "*Yorkshire Pudding*" by Elaine Lemm, a scholarly discourse on the many culinary facets of this most esteemed contribution to the Sunday dinner table. Like the product itself, I find myself wanting a second helping. It is, you'll be fascinated to hear, possible to construct an entire three course meal around the Yorkshire pudding. And who wouldn't choose to end a meal with caramelised apple Yorkshire pudding. Go on, you know you want it. Not quite so sure about the Yorkshire pudding sorbet.

Another book I recently find I like to dip into is "*Canal Narrowboats and Barges*" by Tony Conder, part of that wonderful series of monographs from Shire, a publication house that seems to exist purely to publish affectionate memorabilia in tiny numbers. And who could be unmoved by a publisher with titles like "*Early Electrical Appliances*", "*Straws and Straw Craftsmen*" or their particularly magnificent book on Edwardian perambulators.

Nearer the bottom of the pile is "*The Medici Effect*" by Frans Johansson, a book given to me by The Viking, who assures me that I will be unable to put it down. She's probably right but so far I've been unable to pick it up. I will at some point, and when I do find it as billed, will doubtless get an "I told you so" from The Viking.

But to be honest, the book I find most gripping at present is "*Kamikaze -- Japan's Suicide Samurai*" by Raymond Lamont-Brown. And this really is unputdownable, a gripping, graphic and gruesome analysis of Japan's last throw of the dice in World War II.

So there you have it -- all human life. From the quiet chug chug on rural waterways to the scream of Japanese dive bombers. From the philosophical backwaters of science to the metaphysical magnificence of the Yorkshire pudding.

I can't wait till "*Early Electrical Appliances*" arrives. It'll be just like Christmas.


### 11 January 2012 – Nazis? What Nazis?

Since our visit to Duxford a couple of weeks ago, Alex and I have found a common interest in model aeroplanes. For me this is little more than a rekindling of an old passion from more than forty years ago -- essentially when I was Alex's age. But for Alex, this is new. And from his parents' point of view, welcome relief from the incessant video games.

It goes without saying that putting together model aircraft requires a degree of dexterity that I no longer possess. It's a bit like trying to brush your teeth while wearing boxing gloves. You probably won't get anywhere near teeth, but at least your nostrils will be minty fresh. So I find myself in the role of sage adviser rather than actual technician.

We started with a Sopwith Camel and, despite the relative simplicity of this model, still managed to mislay the undercarriage. Not an auspicious start. Next up was an Apache helicopter gunship. This thing is, in armament terms, a porcupine. In fact I don't know why they didn't call it Porcupine. Positively bristling with guns, missiles and, for all I know, potato peelers and beetroot dicers, this craft is the Swiss Army knife of the helicopter world. There is no end to the creative ways in which it can blow things to smithereens.

Waiting in the wings -- I'm sorry -- are a 1:48 scale Eurofighter and a 1:72 scale Vulcan, advanced level kits that have Alex positively quivering with excitement. You'd think he was a Parky.

But by way of diversion I thought it might be interesting to look at a different sort of aircraft, specifically an airship. I have always been fascinated by the history of airships and thought this might be a welcome change from all the military hardware Alex is determined to construct. It turns out that not a lot of airship models are available, perhaps understandably since, for the most part, they all look the same. But

Revell make a model of the most famous of all dirigibles, LZ 129, the Hindenburg.

The model, thankfully in 1:720 scale, as a 1:72 scale Hindenburg would be the size of a Fiat Punto, is as detailed as one might expect from something that is essentially a flying gherkin. And every one of the albeit few external features, from the gondola to the engine pods, is executed with a fine attention to detail.

All bar one that is. Being essentially the flagship for the German aviation industry in 1936, the zeppelin inevitably carried the swastika on the tailfins. In that respect it was probably no different from any number of other aircraft at that time. Only much bigger.

So when my model of the Hindenburg arrived in the post today, I was surprised to find that the swastika was absent on the tailfins. The white circle on a red background is still present but the swastika has gone AWOL.

Why?

Really why?

Is the world's political stability and security so fragile that a sixty year old symbol less than three millimetres in diameter is too dangerous to print on a historical model? So subversive that some anonymous bureaucrat has sensitively airbrushed it out on our behalf? Will a glimpse of a swastika really fill me with an overwhelming urge to goosestep through Poland (even if I physically could)? If the mere sight of a tiny and -- let's face it -- historically correct detail on a plastic model of an airship is the fast track to totalitarianism, then I'm a banana. There must surely be more conventional means of subversion than this.

I can understand all the sensitivities at play here but I can't help feeling that this sort of "reds under the bed" paranoia is surely misplaced. This is surely censorship gone mad. Hints of Basil Fawlty, and if you ask me. And to think we used to scorn those Soviet pictures of the politburo with members mysteriously absent whenever it suited the current regime.

Note to censor -- common sense please.

Note to self -- time for your medicine. You're beginning to rant.

### 16 January 2012 -- The Salami of Sadness

I've been feeling down for a few days. Nothing I can quite put my finger on, you understand. Just a general feeling of flatness. I am reassured, if that's the word that I'm looking for, that this is not uncommon in Parkinson's.

Still, whether common or not in Parkinson's, it is unusual for me. On the whole, whether I have spent the day pushing paper or wrestling crocodiles (metaphorically), flatness or apathy are quite alien. To me at least.

Depression is nonetheless extraordinarily common in Parkinson's. Estimates vary but it's generally thought that about half of us -- and for the purposes of this discussion, "us" are people with Parkinson's (sorry my healthy friends) -- will experience depression at some point.

But of course depression itself is only one end of a continuum. Closely related psychobiological states include apathy (general disinterest), anhedonia (inability to experience pleasure), dysphoria and goodness knows what else, all part of depression's extended family.

So where does my "general feeling of flatness" fit into this sparkling spectrum of affective disorder?

Am I trying to delude myself into believing that I have clinical depression with all that entails? Or is the opposite true -- that I have a serious illness to which I am rather maladjusted?

Churchill used to talk of his 'Black dog', a prevailing mood of gloom and despondency, during which he would console himself with whisky -- a prescription which I would gladly follow.

Not all self prescribed treatments for depression are quite so life enhancing. Ernest Hemingway struggled with depression in his final years, eventually succumbing to the temptation of a double barrel shotgun. Certainly a decisive solution, even if not a very positive one.

My mother used to suffer from seasonal affective disorder (SAD), long before the name was widely accepted. Always a sun lover, and with a year-round tan to prove it, she found the winter months miserable. From November to February, she was morose and disinterested. Questions which would elicit expansive responses in summer, were dismissed in winter with single words. Sometimes not even that.

I'm not sure that I have SAD and I'm reluctant to endorse my sense of flatness by treating it to one of the existing names. And, I am even more reluctant to give it a new name and thus further slice the salami of sadness.

Besides, it's a feeling of flatness -- like a snooker table -- nothing more. On the whole I'm a great fan of the "snap out of it" school of psychiatry. And if that fails, reach for the shots.

No, I didn't mean those shots Ernie.

## 20 January 2012 - Socks (I think)

If you have just eaten, or are about to eat, you might want to read this later. Or not at all. For reasons which will become clear, my specialist subject this week is canine digestion.

There, I told you to read it later.

Animals on the whole are guided by a food neophobia. In essence they won't eat a new food unless they're confident it is safe. Some animals may take a degree of persuading but it all makes sound evolutionary sense. In essence, the animal assumes something to be dangerous unless shown otherwise. Alex is pretty much the embodiment of this, restricting his diet as much as possible to pizza. You can never be too sure. Better safe than sorry.

Louis -- you remember Louis, our poodle puppy -- seems to have cast aside the lessons from hundreds of millions of years of evolution because, in recent weeks, he has become disturbingly and unpredictably omnivorous. He seems to be guided by the general rule that if it fits in his mouth, it is therefore, by definition, edible. This rule works well with new types of dog food where Louis is more than accommodating. Regrettably, Louis applies the same principles to pieces of tree bark, clothes pegs, Christmas cards and moss.

If we were in some may failing to cater to his dietary needs, this might be understandable. But you would struggle to find a more pampered pup. So this latest predilection is as inexplicable as the diet is inedible. You begin to wonder where he will draw the line. Light bulbs? CDs?

Needless to say, this spontaneous enriching of his diet is accompanied by some extremely unattractive gastrointestinal consequences. In particular, he is sometimes quite eye wateringly flatulent. If he was a kennel-bound outdoor dog, this would pose little problem. But a dog which breaks wind silently in the living room evokes the kind of agonised response from us that would be familiar to anyone who had served on the Western front during the first phosgene attacks of 1915. Only Louis seems impervious to this gaseous sensory assault. The furniture bears the brunt of it. I swear those loose covers have faded more than can be directly attributed to sunlight. .

And if his gastrointestinal assaults ended there, we should count ourselves lucky. Inevitably they don't. Even Louis's cast-iron digestion is occasionally stumped and our evening's television will be interrupted by the sound of a retching dog. On Monday and Tuesday, he generously vomited two socks for us. Both socks, and you will appreciate that I didn't conduct a detailed forensic examination, appeared to have been swallowed whole. More alarmingly, they didn't match, suggesting that further gastric consequences will become apparent.

Louis is a walking vets bill. It can only be a matter of time before even his seemingly impregnable gastrointestinal tract gives up the ghost.

Without dwelling unduly on the subject, nor becoming needlessly scatological, I have to say that I'm equally astonished by the kind of things that pass through our cretinous canine companion. Bits of pinecones and clingfilm are not uncommon. In the post-Christmas period, his motions have occasionally even glittered with tinsel.

And I finally know why our Monopoly set is missing a few hotels.

### 23 January 2012 - Laundry

The weekly wash seems to serve the principal purpose of merely making the male household members feel incompetent. It is an engine of servitude certainly, but not in the obvious direction. We are made to feel especially inadequate because of our inability to correctly match clothing items to their respective owners.

Precisely how am I meant to know that a particular size whatever blouse belongs to Claire, Catherine or Alice? And no, before you start, size is not a reliable indicator. Thus the opportunities for inadvertently causing offence are almost limitless. I think they should just be glad that I can at least narrow it down by gender.

But this slightly haphazard approach, at best inadequate and at worst shambolic, needs replacing with something more systematic. After all, Alex is increasingly expected to take over the mantle (just as well since I've never taken up the mantle in the first place with any kind of seriousness).

But armed with several years of reluctant and marginal sorting of laundry, I have distilled the fruits of my wisdom thus:

Knickers the size of postage stamps are in all probability owned by Alice. Pants the size of a post office will, with equal certainty, be mine.

If the item of clothing is pink, it belongs to Alice. No ifs or buts, Alice is the rightful owner. End of discussion. If it's a black T-shirt emblazoned with skulls, it belongs to Alex. Even Alice during her brief flirtation with the Gothic, drew the line at this sort of grunge. Preppy US college stuff tends to belong to Catherine. Flimsy catwalk stuff belongs to Alice. As for that matter does almost anything with an equine theme. Except, of course, a horse's skull. That will be Alex's -- skulls trump horses every time.

The same kind of rules apply across the board to clothing with pictures. A picture of a bunny could be Alice or Catherine. A pink bunny means Alice. Except where the pink bunny is either (a) saying something rude or (b) decapitated. Then it will be one of the Alex's many 'misunderstood teenager' T-shirts. Like Alex himself, his clothing speaks mostly in grunts.

You get the picture. So it's time for a test. Start with horses?

Four horses in a field – Alice? Yes, for sure.

Four polo ponies – Catherine. Especially if they have fit male riders.

Four horsemen of the apocalypse – Alex.

That was too easy – shall we have a stab at inanimate objects then? Cars?

Pink Figaro with eyelashes – Alice.

Bugatti Veyron – Alex.

Pink Bugatti Veyron – a tough one for Alex. Would his thirst for the very zenith of automotive performance outweigh the inevitability of looking like a complete pilchard? One grunt for yes, two for no.

In any case, this is a side issue. With a young puppy, the washing doesn't get as far as sorting by human hand. Louis, with his own special breed of exuberance, sees to it that all laundry is liberally distributed around the room.

Or, in the case of socks, eaten.

# FEBRUARY

**3 February 2012 - The kindness of strangers**

I arrived at Sevenoaks in plenty of time to catch the 09:19 train, parked the Jag precisely in one of the all too narrow bays and crackled my way over the thick frost to the parking meter. £6.50 for the day -- outrageous by any standard -- but at least a known quantity.

Like all Parkies, I hate fiddling with change. Tremors that are barely ripples in the ether when relaxed, take on an entirely seismic quality when under stress. Such as when fiddling around with change. And I tend to have a lot of change. Mostly this is because I consciously try to avoid situations where I need to rummage in pockets for the odd coin or two. So much easier to pay with a note that you know will be sufficient and deal with the change later.

But on this occasion I had time. And besides, I was only paying a machine not a human being. Nothing to be stressed about. So I had carefully and pre-emptively counted out the correct sum. I should say that this was not achieved without some fidgeting around under the seat, in the glove compartment and ashtray -- all the usual places where money seems, for reasons unfathomable, nonetheless to accumulate. Twenty six 5p pieces, ten 10p coins, a single 20p, two 50p heptagons, a pound and a two pound coin. No less than forty one coins. By the time I had winkled the last florin from the foot well, I was in something of a lather.

Still, no hurry. As I started putting the coins into the meter, I became aware of a couple of people behind me, clearly waiting to use the same meter, and presumably, being able-bodied, having allocated mere nanoseconds to buy their parking ticket before dashing to the train. Inevitably, my hands started to shake and I dropped a coin. But I still had enough and was within 15p of the chequered flag when the machine chose not to accept any more coins from me, a metal bar mysteriously appearing to prevent me doing so. No matter how hard I tried, the path was barred. I tried gentle pushes, petulant thrusts and eventually frustrated punches.

I turned to the man behind me and explained, suggesting at the same time that perhaps he should try his luck. He did. It worked first time. I looked an idiot. I was an idiot -- he told me so. A girl behind him, her iPod sparing her our discussion, entered her coins. Again no problem. I looked like an even bigger idiot. A quivering idiot.

"What's the problem?" she asked, tugging her earphones out. Aware of my writhing tremors, I gave her the short version. She picked the larger denomination coins from my hand and put them into the machine. Then, before I could say anything, she reached into her pocket and inserted two pounds. I gestured to give her my 5p and 10p pieces but she shook her head, gave me a smile that would light up any day, and turned away.

I put my coins back in my pocket and looked up. She was nowhere to be seen.

### 10 February 2012 – Money money money

I'm beginning to understand what it must feel like to have debts so large that default is the only possible option. In other words I feel like Greece. The country that is, and not the John Travolta -- Olivia Newton John smoochfest (I still haven't forgotten Arthur Mullard's version of "You're the one that I want", and infinitely more memorable rendition).

But I digress. Back to the state of insolvency.

Well I'm exaggerating, as usual, but not without cause. Let me explain. The little Merc has become a tad lumpy of late, choosing to hop, skip and jump along the road rather than glide in a manner more befitting the peak of the German automotive engineering. I didn't think much of it at first, putting it down to a dodgy batch of petrol. But as it persisted, and the symptoms intensified, I thought it best to take a look under the bonnet.

This is, as any of my friends will tell you, a supremely pointless undertaking for someone with as little mechanical aptitude as myself. On lifting the bonnet, I was able to satisfy myself that the car had an engine. And that was about as far as my self-reassurance extended. Precisely what I was anticipating, I don't know. Perhaps a large flashing neon sign saying "here is the fault". Or one or two brightly coloured screws that needed tightening. No, none of these. Just an engine. And it is a testament to the depth of my automotive ineptitude that I found even that slightly comforting.

Clearly professional opinion was required. I phoned the garage and with a breezy "it's probably nothing but ..." and offered my description of the symptoms. In fact the words I used to the garage echoed my words to my GP in 2006. I was wrong then, as I was wrong now.

Within an hour of taking the car in, the garage was on the phone. Far from being "probably nothing", it turned out that the little Merc was teetering between life and death. Apparently the fault lay with the EMU which, far from being a large flightless bird, turns out to be an acronym for engine management unit. This is a small electronic module and, much like jewellery, size has little bearing on price. Puny though it may be, the EMU controls pretty much everything to do with engine function

In essence, the car needed a brain transplant. Needless to say, small multifunctional pieces of electronics do not come cheap. And, as the Mercedes garage informed me, they have to be tailor-made for each individual car (no really, that's what they said). And that means that this thing had to be made in Stuttgart.

Rather like a cartoon character, I can see £ signs flashing in front of my eyes. Just how much is a bespoke German brain going to set me back, I ask. The mechanic pretends to flick nonchalantly through the catalogue before alighting on the correct product code. The sound of air being sucked through teeth confirms my worst fears.

"Well" he says "do you want the part fitted?"

"No " I say "I will wear it as a necklace"

You're right -- I didn't say that but I thought it. What other possible alternatives would there be? Of course I want the b****y thing fitted. If it's not too much trouble.

Anyway, to cut a long story short, the part in question (fitted) plus a couple other minor knicknacks comes to the eye watering sum of £1731. My first reaction was to enquire whether he was familiar with decimals and if not, to make double sure the decimal point was in the right place. It turned out it was. My second reaction was to ask him how much the car itself was worth. About the same as the repairs apparently.

After a little further exchange of banter, he let slip that the car was not roadworthy in its present state and that the garage would be resistant to me driving it away without the work being done. In the space of less than an hour the car had gone, in automotive terms, from a tickle at the back of the throat to terminal lung cancer and my credit card was now in a full-blown hostage situation.

A week later, and the car is back. Polished too. And I have to say that its new brain is a darned sight brighter than its old brain. The car glides along now. Which just leaves me a couple of weeks before the credit card bill arrives...

Keep calm and carry on.

### 17 February 2012 – "4403"

In one of those idle moments one sometimes conjures from nothing, most often when one has a very pressing something to do, I found my mind wandering. Specifically I asked myself how many doses of medicine had I taken since being diagnosed with PD? The answer, as you doubt is gleaned from the title of this, is 4403. That includes everything prescribed for me - rotigotine, levodopa, propranolol and rasagiline -- but not those pills I prescribe for myself -- vitamin E, ginkgo biloba and occasional Q10.

Putting all these prescribed tablets and capsules together, they would fill a good-sized sweet jar. You know, the kind they had in confectioners when we were young, full of sherbet lemons or flying saucers. That's not bad for five years.

Laid end to end, the tablets and capsules would form a line 27.64 metres long, the distance from our back door to the end of our garden and back, even allowing for a detour around the chicken coop. Add another five years of treatment at, in all probability, increasing doses, and my medication will stretch like some pill popping python around the neighbour's house and back. And who knows where the medicines will get to over a longer period of time.

If you added the various self prescribed medicines/food supplements/snake oil that I also take, then this anaconda of additives would stretch to the next road junction. I kid you not. And don't forget that, in relation to many other Parkies, my medication list is relatively modest.

And as for those rotigotine patches, I calculated that the area covered over the last five years is 7.88 square metres or, put another way, the area of approximately 2 king-size double duvets (and I'm all for the king-size double duvet to become the new SI unit).

But even so, I calculate that I've drunk four hundred and thirty eight litres of water purely to wash down my tablets. That's essentially two baths full or, to my parents who lived through years of wartime deprivation, nearer ten.

To be honest, and it's probably a reflection of my perceived tendency to exaggerate, I had rather hoped that the tablets might extend to the nearest village, that the patches might cover a football field and that the volume of water might fill an Olympic swimming pool. But if that were the case I suspect I would be dead. Or, at the very least, wrapped up in patches tied with tablet strings, like a quivering latter-day Harry Houdini.

Of course you can get fixated on this sort of trivia. Obsessive even. But then the male of the species has always been a little bit nerdy when it comes to numbers and bizarre facts -- a pregnant goldfish is called a twit. Scissors were invented by Leonardo da Vinci. More people are killed by donkeys each year than are killed in plane crashes. John Lennon's first girlfriend was named Thelma Pickles. And the average human inhales about 700,000 of their own skin flakes each day.

Okay so the last paragraph probably didn't only dispel the nerdy obsessive tag. Still I should like to point out that this is an isolated incident and not a harbinger of psychological gloom. More an idle sort of parlour game than a withdrawal into navelgazing obsession. Simply haven't got time for that.

And talking of time, did you know that a jiffy is one hundredth of a second.

OK, I'll get my coat.

### 21 February 2012 – Tossers

In days gone by, the act of calling your parent a tosser might be expected to have one's father reaching for his belt, slipper, newspaper or whatever came immediately to hand. Tom Hay, unequivocally the naughtiest boy in our school, was constantly being punished by parents, teachers and shopkeepers for misdemeanours that ranged from pulling his sister's pigtails, through a catalogue of other indeterminate atrocities, to shoplifting armfuls of Curly Wurlies. His posterior had, over many years of misdemeanours, being the recipient of attention from slippers, bare hands, canes, and even on one occasion a pair of novelty salad tongs, the handle of which his father had mistaken for his walking stick.

It was little better at school where Tom had set, and for all I know still holds, an unenviable variety of disciplinary records -- most times caned (eleven), most consecutive terms caned (five), shortest interval between canings (six hours), most consecutive strokes of the cane (eight -- should have been six but the headmaster was distracted by a phone ringing). If getting into trouble was an Olympic sport, the hottest cert for a gold this summer would not be Usain Bolt.

Tom never really grasped the "this will hurt me far more than it hurts you" line popular with teachers and headmasters of that era. If it was so darned painful, why did they subject themselves to such needless suffering, he reasoned, even offering to cane the headmaster in one brief moment of misplaced logical clarity.

Of course those days are gone. Canes gather dust in the attic, slippers have been chewed to death by the dog, and the whereabouts of the novelty salad tongs is anybody's guess. But on this occasion being called "a great tosser" by Alex evoked pleasant memories rather than a need to deploy a punitive arsenal.

Before the onset of Parkinson's, I had indeed been a great tosser.

No matter how large, thick or adhesive the pancake, I could make it execute barrel rolls, flips and pirouettes before depositing it safely back in the pan on the reverse side. Nowadays the pancakes will just as confidently end up on the floor, microwave oven, draining board or even Louis. That insidious loss of fine motor control, witnessed in our scratchy handwriting, means that I will not pick up the pan. But whereas Claire is of the old school and able to perform triple somersaults with ease, the same cannot be said of the kids. It has to be said, but my children are a useless bunch of tossers.

## 25 February 2012 – My PC has PD

I think my PC is going to have to go to the doctors. It's been getting progressively worse for some six months or so. Programs crash, the soundcard stutters, and sometimes the whole thing just grinds to a halt or finds itself locked in some vortex of unproductive activity, the hard disk sounding like a butterfly in a matchbox.

This processing bradykinesia has been present for a while now. I keep thinking it will improve, and sometimes briefly it does, but these are little more than the flickering embers of its former self. So what do you think is wrong with it? Let's look at the symptoms. Slow thinking, takes ages to complete tasks it should be able to do instantly, tendency to get stuck and unable to start moving again. Oh and the CD drive makes the whole computer shake.

So there's the clinical picture -- slow thinking, slow-moving, tremors and stiffness. Ring any bells?

Now I think about it, the PC has probably had PD for quite awhile. This pre-diagnostic phase has gone on for nearly a year. Looking back some of the symptoms are obvious. The PC has become more introspective, less attentive to me. Whereas before it would translate every word I dictated into text on the page with hardly a pause for breath, in the last few months, it has seemed strangely distracted, difficult to engage and self absorbed.

So where do we go from here? Add in more memory chips perhaps. A new graphics accelerator then. More disk space maybe. And like the real medicines and neurological tinkering we undergo, the results would produce sharp improvements for a while, only to be replaced by deterioration's inexorable march. Each CPU upgrade on the computer would buy a little more valuable time and functionality. And we would be thankful for that in the same way we are for the drugs that improve our own CPu. But in the end, the CPU on the computer (Central Processor Unit) would, like our own CPu (caudate-putamen), reached the point where no modifications would still work.

And perhaps that's the point. That all this tinkering around the periphery is nothing more than a way of buying time. Nothing more than treading water until, by hope or design, a cure appears. And whilst we are grateful for the ability to stay in the water, it's not an end in itself.

Don't get me wrong -- I'm as grateful as the next man for the treatments which help me get out of bed in the morning and still my shakes. Really I am. But to be honest, I'm a little less grateful this year than I was last. And in turn I was a little less grateful last year than the one before. I hate to look a gift horse in the mouth, but I'm beginning to wonder if I shouldn't expect more. Maybe just say "thanks for the horse, get back to me when you've made a reasonable stab at the internal combustion engine". Do you get my point? We have to move away from simply buying time. Time is important only if there is realistic hope of a cure at the end. And I want more than just time. I want to know that one day this will be lifted from my shoulders.

My computer is reaching the point where no further modifications will help. Any further treatment is palliative. The PC technicians have nothing more to offer my near bedridden computer. They shake their heads and point me to the shelves of glittering new computers.

I know exactly what they mean.

## 28 February 2012 – Chairman MAO-B

Like many of the more perky Parkies, I have been taking Azilect as part of my daily smorgasbord of medicines. This is based on the certain hope (if perhaps less certain evidence) that it may be neuroprotective and slow down the progression of the Parkinson's. It doesn't seem to do much symptomatically for me but who cares -- as long as it is protecting that last tender handful of dopamine neurons, that's fine. And for the most part, it is largely free of side-effects -- for me at least. We'll know whether it works or not in five years and so but it seems a good each way bet. So I happily pop the pills every morning with barely a second thought.

But this week is different. Because this week I have managed to catch the family cold. The kids seem to be largely immune, suffering only minor headaches and runny noses. Claire was in bed for nearly five days such was its virulence. And the little blighter appears to have lost none of its potency in crossing to my side of the bed. My nose is a scale model of Niagara and I sneeze with all the force of field artillery. Handkerchiefs are swiftly rendered beyond redemption and I trail tissues around the house like an Andrex puppy. Even the technology is abandoning me. The voice recognition software, comfortable with my clearly enunciated vowels and consonants, is clearly not expecting Melvyn Bragg.

Under normal circumstances, a slug of Night Nurse would swiftly put me back on the road to recovery -- as opposed to the highway to hell my symptomatology comfortably manifests. But there's the problem. If you stop to read the blurb on these tablets, printed in microscopically small lettering, you will could be alerted to the fact that one should not take decongestants if you are also popping Azilect pills. And with good reason.

Okay, a bit of science. Skip the next paragraph or so if you are already yawning. The main constituent of Azilect is a drug called rasagiline and its mode of action is to block monoamine oxidase or MAO as it is more commonly known (nothing to do with former Chinese leaders by the way). MAO normally breaks down dopamine so blocking it means more dopamine available to the neurons. With me so far? Well, as it happens MAO comes in two flavours named with egregious lack of imagination MAO-A and MAO-B. Old-fashioned antidepressants mostly block the A form while rasagiline mainly blocks B.

Back to the Night Nurse. Night Nurse, well pretty much all cold and flu remedies it has to be said, contains a decongestant. And decongestants are broken down by -- you've guessed it -- MAO. On the whole, they tend to be broken down by MAO-A. But if you're taking one of the old style antidepressants, the decongestant gets into the bloodstream and into the brain and causes huge release of catecholamines. Now among the other things that I mean do is raise blood pressure. So a big release of catecholamines causes a big increase in blood pressure. And I'm not talking here about a little bit of a headache. I'm talking about the kind of increase in blood pressure that causes strokes and heart attacks. Short of blasting the top of your head off like a soup bowl, it's hard to see how they could be more dangerous.

But rasagiline blocks MAO-B, I hear you say. Why the worry? Well, it probably isn't a major worry but it's worth remembering that no drug is truly specific for one receptor. And although rasagiline is pretty good, you cannot rule out the possibility that there will be some MAO-A blockade. I'm taking no chances. So, without decongestants, the cold lasts longer and will be more severe. Why settle for a mere cold thinks the virus. Let's shoot for lobar pneumonia.

Still, better safe than sorry. Besides, we already have enough soup bowls.

# MARCH

## 9 March 2012 – Better

I cannot abide whingers. My feeling is that there is a certain type of person who, if blessed with little to whinge about, will nonetheless contrive to find some crumb of discomfort worthy of wider dissemination. You know the type. Always some ache or pain to amplify out of all proportion. Always, like dementors, draining the happiness from those around them. Glasses half empty.

My parents taught me very early on that the answer to the question "how are you?" was always a hearty "very well thank you". This was a rigid commandment, based on the premise that if you whined about nothing, the Almighty would feel compelled to fill that void for you with something very real to complain over.

So the answer was always "very well thank you". It mattered not one jot whether you were peppered with cankers, sores and buboes, and burning up with a kind of fever that would fry eggs. The answer was still "very well thank you". If you wanted to extend the ultimate courtesy, you would add the words "and you?". As with the initial enquiry, etiquette demanded that the interlocutor reciprocate with "very well thank you". This is the kind of stiff upper lip that built the British Empire (and, for that matter, lost it but we'll gloss over that), the kind of colonial *sang froid* that coloured in half the globe in imperial colours.

I remember, as a small child, being bewildered by one of my father's patients, an old lady, who responded to my earnest enquiry with a long and unexpected soliloquy about the ravages of her lumbago. I stood openmouthed. My bewilderment was further confounded by my complete lack of knowledge of lumbago. Somehow at the back of my mind I thought it was a river in Africa and, although she was evidently a woman of learning, knowledgeable and worldly, it didn't seem to be the kind of thing that should cause Mrs Hepplewhite the kind of anguish that it evidently did. Why precisely should a river 3000 miles away have her tossing and turning all night long? It just didn't make sense. But then I was only five and it would be another decade before I knew the difference between the musculoskeletal disorder that kept Agnes Hepplewhite awake in the wee hours (lumbago) and the crocodile-filled river delta in Mozambique (Limpopo).

In any case why couldn't she just have said "very well thank you".

Which is of course exactly what I should have said, in the context of last week's extended rhapsody on a theme of colds and monoamine oxidase. Still, I threw in some science so you weren't shortchanged. In any case, my cold, or man flu or whatever, has abandoned its malign grip on me. Part of this I ascribe to my enthusiastic substitution of malt whisky for Night Nurse in the fulminant phase of the cold. Well, all phases actually. Armed with this chemical cosh, I have slept soundly. Which is more than can be said for Claire, her slumber assailed by the kind of snoring that rattles windows in their casements and moves ornaments along shelves. This is not well received. When a particularly seismic snore jerks me into consciousness, Claire is already wide awake, playing solitaire on the iPhone. The alarm clock kick starts the day. Radio 4 is discussing the latest scientific findings on sacroiliac degeneration.

That's lumbago to you and me.

## 21 March 2012 – Planes, trains and automobiles

It has been one of those weeks when I completely lose track of where I am or where I'm meant to be. I remember getting up very early on Wednesday morning to catch the Eurostar to Brussels. I also remember getting in the car and turning the ignition key. The next thing I can clearly remember was switching off the engine at Ebbsfleet. The journey, some 40 minutes or 30 miles of excruciating motorway boredom (at a steady sixty nine and three quarter miles per hour, officer) had clearly barely tickled my mind into consciousness. For many, 40 minutes of apparent unconsciousness would seem to be the ideal way of tackling the M25. Even so, as an indicator of general cerebral function, that's not very encouraging. You begin to wonder what else you missed in that lost 40 minutes.

I have to admit that I have a real trainspotter fondness for the Eurostar. Firstly it is incredibly fast, a feat achieved without instability. It's hard to imagine any other environment in which one can drink a cup of coffee at 200 miles an hour without fear of spillage. Try that in a motorcar and the interior will smell of Starbucks forever. Secondly, being full of mainly business people, the carriage is relatively quiet. The only voices belong to the usual Gordon Gecko types who believe that the whole world needs to know about the position they had taken that day on Panamanian zinc or something similar. Apart from their isolated braying, the train is silent. Especially on the early morning trains, the occasional ringtone or clink of coffee cups are the only sounds. Thirdly, the blessed thing runs on time, which is more than can be said for much of the remainder of the chemins de fer crisscrossed by the mighty Eurostar.

Before I have too much of a Ronnie Corbett distractionfest moment, let's return to the train, as I did many hours later once the meeting had ended. A white knuckle ride to the train station in the back of Patrick's Mercedes and, by the time I had regained my composure, the Eurostar was well on its way back to Blighty. Patrick has something of a reputation in the company where he works, backed up by his ability to drive at extraordinarily high speeds while maintaining a distance of about a metre from the car in front. It's hard to avoid a sort of grudging admiration, whilst still threading rosary beads through one's fingers. Even in Belgium they called him The Stig. I asked one of his colleagues why he drove so fast. Too much espresso seemed to be the consensus view.

Any time saved by Patrick's attempts to set a new land speed record was lost by the Eurostar being frisked for stowaways just north of Lille although, in the end, we were only marginally late arriving at Ebbsfleet. Incidentally, and I'm not complaining since its location suits me very well, who thought of putting an international railway station in the middle of nowhere (apart from Northfleet and the less said about that the better probably)?

I have hardly had time to down a Red Bull before I'm back in the car and heading towards Gatwick. M25 traffic is a lot less agreeable at 5:30 on a Wednesday afternoon then at 5.30 on a Tuesday morning. The deserted roads of the early morning bear no relation to the frenetic Keystone Cops-style interweaving of traffic in the twilight. Maybe Patrick isn't quite so bad after all.

I am checked in at the Norwegian Air desk by the blondest girl I have ever seen. Almost white. But that wasn't the only surprise. It turns out that Norwegian aircraft have WiFi. How cool is that! By the time the plane lands at Arlanda, I have done all my e-mails for the day. In any case it is already tomorrow when I clear customs. I check into the 'Rest and Fly' hotel in terminal five. Cheap and cheerful is how it is billed, although both 'cheap' and 'cheerful' have different meanings in Scandinavia. And since the hotel room has no window, the absence of light and sound means that I sleep like a baby for the first time in weeks. It is like one of those sensory deprivation experiments popular with 1970s psychologists and members of The Grateful Dead. Probably good training since I'm off to the Karolinska in the morning. Three cheers for Swedish coffee.

### 24 March 2012 – Big phone

Every once in a while, my mobile phone company lets me upgrade my phone for free, or something similar to free. I think all phone companies do. So every two years I'm faced with a couple of webpages full of spanking new phones about which I know nothing but from which I am nonetheless expected to make an intelligent choice.

A few years back the choice would have been easy -- I would simply have picked the most expensive, fastest, swankiest, cleverest phone available on the pitiful grounds that (a) it was free and (b) this would impress my friends. Pathetic really. And on the whole my friends were unimpressed, correctly seeing through this rather repulsive display of greed.

In those days it seemed that less was more, in the sense that the smaller the phone the greater the cachet. Something the size of a postage stamp was infinitely superior to anything larger. Small was beautiful. But to me it seemed at odds with one of the basic facts of anatomy -- the mouth is a good 6 inches (sorry 15 cm) from the ear and since it's necessary to use both organs when on the phone, any telephone which has a microphone and speaker separated by a distance substantially less than this seems doomed to failure. Unless of course the manufacturers are looking to corner the midget market. When I say that both the mouth and ears are necessary for any telephone conversation, I am of course overlooking the brain that evolution has developed to link these two organs. Although anyone who has overheard a post-prandial mobile phone conversation between two merchant bankers would freely acknowledge that the use of brain to link ears and mouth is not a universal evolutionary phenomenon.

Still, failing to recognise that these were indeed the emperor's new clothes, I have plumped for the least plump phone each year. And each year my friends have, through rictus smiles, oooohed and aaaahed at the right points when I reeled off a litany of features the offending article possessed. And gradually, year on year, I have found it a little more difficult to use this micro phone. My fingers are fatter, my eyesight poorer and my tremor coarser. So at every upgrade it has been a question of whether this pathophysiological full house will be trumped by vanity.

I'm pleased to report that, as of yesterday, those days are over. There is little point in having a phone the size of my index finger. Nor is any display the size of a thumbnail much use when it is held at arm's length. Nor is the conventional touchscreen much use when the tremor is in full flow. One exaggerated shiver whilst answering a text from my aunt and I find I have functionally disinherited myself.

The solution in question, and the final nose thumbing victory over vanity, is a Samsung Galaxy Note, a phone the size of a ping-pong table. Or so I'm told by my friends, finally venting from those years of barely suppressed irritation. Well it may not be quite that big but I can see the keys, press the keys and make phone calls with ease. Also my texts and e-mails are now written in English instead of the Swahili into which my arms length typing had evolved. So I'm happy to put up with the laughter of my friends as I hold this tea tray of a phone to my head. It's worth it just to be able to make calls.

In any case, I don't know what my friends are fussing about. The phone is still small enough to fit into a trouser pocket. Although of course you do have to wear the special trousers.

### 27 March 2012 – Duty free

Any seasoned traveller will tell you that a duty free shop, despite the alluring displays and promised savings, will actually do the opposite. You will not come away from the shop thinking how much you've saved. And this rule holds everywhere in the world. All duty-free shops cost you a significant amount of money. And nowhere is that more true than in Sweden. Wherever I travel, especially if it's a favourite country -- as Sweden has become for me -- I like to bring home some sort of memento, usually edible. And if possible I like to find something slightly out of the ordinary. A bit quirky. So having spent the entire week at a conference and therefore unable to shop, it was the usual last-minute rush to find something appropriate. And when I say last-minute, it doesn't get more last-minute than duty-free at Arlanda. In terms of gifts for the family, this really is the last chance saloon. And don't they know it.

The scene panned out pretty much as you would imagine. Five minutes before they closed my gate for the flight and I'm faced with either picking up a family sized box of nougat on arrival at Gatwick (which, let's face it, will fool nobody that it is authentically Scandinavian) or buying something here. I instantly rule out the gravadlax on the grounds that I can pick that up in Sainsbury's. In any case I will probably be accused of having done so anyway. Glass is the same deal. Beautiful certainly and authentically Swedish. But also available in IKEA. As the tannoy calls for the last remaining passengers, I grab the first thing that looks remotely plausible, swiftly hand over my credit card, then make a dash - to strangers, a sort of accelerated waddle -- to the departure gate. In my haste I have bought a piece of moose.

That's right -- moose.

Or more specifically, smoked moose. It was only when I got the thing home (the thing being a piece of smoked moose the size of a child's fist) that I realised how expensive it was. Two hundred and twenty Swedish crowns seemed a pretty decent price at the time. I was the other side of the departure gate at Arlanda before I realised that there are in fact ten crowns to the pound and not 100 as I had erroneously assumed. Somehow I had managed to pay £22 for a small chunk of a very large animal. On a pound per pound (or kilogram per crown) basis, the moose was about the same price as gold leaf. No wonder the girl behind the counter gave me one of those "are you absolutely seriously wanting to buy this? This is insanely expensive and only the fact that you are a tourist prevents me from pointing this out" looks. In return I cast her a "I am a dumb tourist who probably has gullible across his forehead. Please feel free to abuse my wallet in any meaningful way you see fit." There's no denying that Sweden is an expensive country. But I had no idea that leaving it would be even more costly. Still I did leave the country in one piece which is more can be said for the moose. Or my credit card.

# APRIL

**1 April 2012 - Surprise!**

It is six thirty in the morning and Rollo is snoring in the next room. I am wide awake as the grey subtleties of approaching dawn let me rise without need for explanation. I have slept for perhaps three hours. A comfortable bed and a belly full of tortillas and St Emilion have still not aided my sleep. Nor did the in depth comparison of the many merits of Talisker and Ardbeg, a discussion we punctuated with more drams than is healthy (how big is a dram anyway?).

For Rollo and JR this has had the effect of a chemical cosh as neither are moving. Rollo is at least in the recovery position. But for me, Mr Happy Pills, there is no such call to the chambers of Morpheus. The light is changing and, on a sudden whim, I rise, throw on a jumper over my pyjamas and climb out onto the roof patio to watch the dawn. A bat flutters noiselessly by and, for a moment, I half expect to see Christopher Lee materialise in the mist slowly drifting across the valley. But I am alone. This is my time. The first sliver of sun breaks the horizon and in my head I hear Brunnhilde singing "Heil dir sonne...."

Dawn is fast in Malta. We are some fifteen degrees further south and the dawn does not linger in the way of the Scandinavian or Northern European sunup. In what feels like seconds it is done and the occasional car becomes a solid drone of traffic.

Malta? Rollo? JR? I'd better backtrack a bit.

JR, one of my oldest friends (properly that should be 'friend of long standing') turns 50 this weekend and Juliet, JR's infinitely tolerant partner, has A Plan. Never was the term 'better half' more apposite than for Juliet. Juliet has arranged a surprise for JR. Rollo and I are to come out to Malta for the weekend, surprising JR at the end of the working day, because it is a dead cert that JR will be caught unawares. And so it proves. Months of careful planning culminate in Rollo and I emerging from behind a curtain shouting 'Surprise!' a single word that, although effective, so completely undersells the infinite subterfuge and deception that has underpinned this endeavour. JR, who has spent the last eleven hours wrestling with hedge fund management, is, as predicted, utterly wrongfooted, emitting a sound that has divided opinion. Rollo says it was a yelp but, for me, it was nearer a whimper.

The best part, all captured on video, is the sight of Juliet smiling the smile of Hannibal (think 'A Team' not 'Silence of The Lambs') and watching with satisfaction as the plan has finally come together. Game, set and match to Juliet.

## 4 April 2012 – Pirates of the Mediterranean

The first phase of Juliet's plan, ably executed by Rollo and I, had so completely fooled JR that his guard was down. For JR, this was the surprise. His oldest friends had come to see him. He saw no reason to believe otherwise and we saw no reason to help him realise the main event was yet to come. This was just the overture.

The main event in question was an infinitely more elaborate subterfuge. Unbeknownst to JR, Juliet had assembled a hundred of his friends at a secret location, for a party. Friends from work, Britain, Malta, sporting friends, every walk of life. Saturday night was all arranged. All we had to do was keep this secret from JR from Thursday until Saturday evening when we would take JR out for 'a quiet meal' at a waterfront restaurant. Upon arrival, the guests would spring out to surprise JR, while I charged the defibrillator.

The venue for this deception was The Black Pearl, and this is not your average restaurant. Because the Black Pearl started life in Pukavik in 1909 as a wooden schooner carrying grain, coal and wood, to remote areas of Norway and Sweden. And if her timbers could speak, this ship would have a story to tell. After surviving two world wars she was briefly Errol Flynn's private yacht before becoming a luxury passenger vessel in the 1970s, based in Melbourne. Not a bright idea. After developing weevil worm she was despatched to Blighty for urgent repairs.

Unfortunately, damage sustained from a fire in the engine room as she traveled through the Suez Canal, sank her in Marsamxett harbour. End of story you might think.

Actually no. In 1979, she was raised and restored, thus beginning a glittering cinema career of, well, two films - 'Popeye' and (more recently) one of the Pirates of The Caribbean set. She sank again in a storm in 1981 and was again refloated. This time she was sensibly taken out of the water, plonked down on the Ta' Xbipex quayside and turned into a restaurant and bar in 1987.

Back to the party. A minibus arrived for us at seven thirty. The guests were already ensconced and plied with Sangria. When our bus arrived at the Black Pearl, the lookout sounded the alert and all hid in the stern like naughty schoolboys. We climbed the stairs and, for the second time in forty eight hours, JR was given the shock of his life. This time it was a definite yelp, a sound that I'll warrant many of his business friends, including a member of the Maltese parliament, had not heard before.

It is fair to say that the Maltese know how to party. Let's face it, any nation that has received the George Cross has got the right stuff. And what are a few tequila slammers compared with the might of the Luftwaffe. These are strong people and they know how to let their hair down.

It is also fair to say that I saw a side to my daughters I had not previously experienced. While Rollo and I had watched the cricket at Marsa, Juliet had taken the girls shopping. If the George Cross was ever to be awarded for fashion, Alice would unquestionably be a recipient. Even Juliet was stunned by the intensity of the shopathon to which she was mercilessly subjected by my girls.

The fruits of this retail therapy were at least partly manifested in the form of a pair of 8 inch heels for Alice, bringing her up to Catherine's height of nearly six feet. So attired, it is fair to say that the girls created something of a stir on the dance floor, teaching the locals a number of moves they had probably never seen before. Most had names that cannot be written here - this is a family show. And if their presence on the dance floor was cyclonic, their work at the bar with the shot glasses was even more jawdropping.

The following morning I had a headache. The girls had fifty new Facebook friends and more texts than I receive in a year.

### 6 April 2012 – Hydrogen

You will remember an earlier rant about a model of the Hindenburg that I was making and the absence of historically accurate detail. Fret not - I'm not going to open up that can of worms. But, being naturally obsessive, I found it aroused my interest. Mainly, I suppose because there is nothing similar to an airship today. Like the Concorde, the airships represent a bygone age of air travel. Whereas the Concorde was predicated on the notion of speed – "Breakfast in London, Lunch in New York (Luggage in Bahrain)" – the airships took a more relaxed, leisurely approach, crossing the oceans like liners. Indeed they were the original air-liners at a time when transatlantic aeroplanes really didn't exist.

But most impressive of all was the sheer size of the ships. The Graf Zeppelin was 776 feet long, twice the length of a football pitch. Stood on its end it was most of the height of the Empire State building. Capable of eighty mph, it had a usable payload of fifteen tons. That's an awful lot of bratwurst.

And this was an age of luxury. Zeppelin passengers had hot and cold running water in their centrally heated and cooled cabins. Passengers were still advised to carry a light overcoat on board and men were told that a comfortable cap was a good idea too. In the same way that baggage is weighed nowadays, so it was then. Because weight was critical. The zeppelins even took into account the number of male or female passengers since a man's suit would often weigh as much as ten dresses. But such calculations were done discreetly, as befits such a luxurious mode of travel. Fortunately in those days there were no name and shame budget airlines.

But this was very much luxury travel. Each zeppelin had two observation decks, a restaurant and a saloon that, despite the weight premium, still found space for a grand piano. But even the piano had to lose some weight. Constructed mostly of aluminium, it tipped the scales at a mere one hundred and eighty kilogrammes. It is reflection of the age that a grand piano was considered an essential cultural accoutrement rather than extravagant frippery.

This was café society, an age when men were expected to dress for dinner. Dinner, served on bone china, might be black forest trout followed by venison cutlets, washed down with fine French and German wines. The galley kitchen on board catered for nearly ninety passengers and crew. Fresh bread was baked daily.

After dinner of course one might feel like a cigar. So, more surprising even than the piano, was the presence on board of a smoking room, a feature that seems to sit uncomfortably with the adjacent presence of four million cubic feet of hydrogen. Hydrogen, as any schoolboy will tell you, is not just flammable. It is explosive. And, as anyone who has seen the famous footage of the Hindenburg disaster will attest, it all burns pretty darned quickly. One spark and poof! Unsurprisingly passengers were politely requested not to carry matches or automatic lighters on airships. The lighters in the smoking room were, like hotel keys, too large to be pocketed. In any case, they were chained to the tables.

But of course the zeppelins had a much more chequered history. Although originally designed for carrying passengers, the German military swiftly recognised the potential of airships as war machines. And for much of the First World War, the zeppelins served as long-range bombers. And pretty rubbish they were too. Once the Royal Air Force wised up to tracer ammunition, the zeppelins were doomed. After all, you don't need to be much of a marksman to be able to hit a bag of hydrogen a quarter of a mile across. Nearly three quarters of all the zeppelins used in the First World War were shot down. Casualties amongst zeppelin air crew were higher than those on the ground.

Their use as war machines led in turn directly to the Hindenburg disaster. Because the Hindenburg, unlike its immediate predecessor was designed to be filled with helium, which provided much of the buoyancy of hydrogen, but without that unfortunate habit of bursting into flames. In the early Thirties however, the United States more or less controlled world supplies of helium. If you weren't friends with Uncle Sam, you had no helium.

And the US were more than a tad uncomfortable with the German administration at the time. All those strange goosestepping chappies with their funny crosses. So they had no helium, and were compelled against their better judgement to fill the Hindenburg with hydrogen. That alone shouldn't have created a problem. As long as it is contained, and people aren't firing machine guns at it, hydrogen is fine. The problem with the Hindenburg lay not so much with the content as the covering. In order to prevent the gas cells overheating, the Hindenburg was painted with a reflective waterproof paint. Made of a mixture of aluminium, nitrates and cellulose acetate butyrate, this coating was highly flammable. One electrical spark and poof!

But on the whole, and the Hindenburg disaster notwithstanding, airship travel was surprisingly safe. When it was finally retired, the Graf Zeppelin had made five hundred and ninety flights, a hundred and forty three transatlantic crossings, and notched up more than a million miles carrying thirteen thousand one hundred and ten passengers in supreme luxury. Today we have Ryanair. Tell me that's progress.

## 10 April 2012 – Cricket!

Hard to believe when it is so cold, wet and miserable (we had hail today) but the cricket season is upon us. As regular readers know, I love the game of cricket, its infinite complexities, twists, subtleties and nuances. I love the ebb and flow of the game and the rhythm and balance.

Last season was magical. For the first time, Alex played a complete season – previous years have ended early with broken limbs – and he really came of age as a bowler, breaking several records. I'm sorry for those uninterested in cricket, but I would be neglecting my duties as Proud Dad if I failed to list them – forty four wickets at eleven runs apiece and two hat tricks, his first senior hat trick (all bowled), youngest hat trick taker in our club's history, best bowling performance (seven for eight off seventeen balls) in the history of his junior league at any age, top all time wicket taker in the junior league, and best junior bowling figures in our club's history. I hope I didn't miss any.

These peaks in his bowling were more or less mirrored by the troughs in my batting. After a single unexpectedly decent knock of twenty seven in the pre-season, I accumulated only nine more runs in a further twelve innings for the 4th XI, with eight ducks. Despite this overwhelming evidence to the contrary, I am optimistic about the new season. And this season, once again, I am like a little schoolboy. I am more excited than any unfit, overweight fifty four year old man has the right to be. I can't wait to get out there and feel that buzz. The first friendlies start next weekend. Alex and I have put our names down and should know by Wednesday if we are picked.

It's ridiculous really. I am in poorer shape than ever before, unlikely to make a contribution with bat or ball and desperately short of net practice. But at least my bat is oiled and my kit is sorted. I have even emptied out my cricket bag of extraneous paraphernalia in preparation for the new season. I initially thought the waft of mustiness that greeted me was just the smell of my cricket shoes but a more detailed examination traced the source to a mummified cheese and ham baguette. The sell by date, only just readable, was 9th September 2011.

These are not good signs. But I am taking action. No, not about the baguette. The batting, I mean. I am having a few coaching sessions.

Now I don't delude myself that I will turn into Alastair Cook overnight, transmogrified from ultimate village cricket bunny into test match run machine. But, let's face it, any improvement would be worthwhile. And my objectives are modest – not centuries or even fifties. Not even the acquisition of new strokes. No, my aim is simple - I just want to stay in for longer. Let others get the runs.

And that means mastering only one stroke – the forward defensive. Chris, our head coach tells me of one (unnamed) player at the club who has only one attacking shot. But (s)he has mastered the forward defensive. For most of each over (s)he waits patiently, comfortably blocking each delivery until the bad ball comes, as come it must in village cricket, and (s)he can slash it to the boundary. Even with this limited arsenal of shots, the player comfortably accumulates runs. The key to it all, is not to get out. You can't score runs in the pavilion.

I have a further incentive. Hard to believe (and a decision almost certainly made for non-cricket reasons) but I have been made 4th XI skipper this season. I will never be the sort of swashbuckling captain, leading from the front with huge flowing innings. But I would like to be able to anchor an end. Last season Alex took more wickets than I scored runs. That's the first thing I have to change.

Well, the second. The ham and cheese baguette is making a run for it.

## 18 April 2012 – Chi Chi

The girls are back from their skiing holiday. All thanks to my eldest. Catherine, and it always seems to be Catherine, is one of those people that seem to be at the centre of things. When, as a youngster, she went to the summer residential music courses in Kent, she was the girl that everyone else wanted to share a dormitory with. And it was always for the same reason "because things happen around Catherine". Whether it was sneaking chocolate bars from the canteen in the middle of the night or water bombing the boys' dormitory, whatever the mischief I would have the feeling that my daughter was not far away.

Things do happen around Catherine. And she does seem to have that happy knack of being in the right place at the right time. In this case, she had filled out a competition entry form in a magazine with her name and e-mail address. A month later, a phone call from the organisers told her she had won a short break skiing holiday in Chamonix. For four people. Staying at The Clubhouse. With two hundred and fifty pounds of winter clothing for each person. And a thousand pounds of spends. No catches.

Mind you, in a resort which charges seven euros for a bottle of Evian, the grand doesn't go as far as it might elsewhere. This is, after all, where the Royals go to ski. Especially when they don't want to be bothered by the riffraff. Chamonix is the kind of place where a couple of glasses of gluhwein will put a hole in your wallet the size of Antarctica. A place where you carry bullion rather than credit cards. Bearing in mind that snow is just frozen water, it's surprising that the enterprising burghers of Chamonix have not found a way of charging for that as well. Although, in essence of course, they have. A ski pass costs as much as a family hatchback.

Despite the fact that the average age of the party was twenty, and that Alice, the undisputed queen of the slammer, was with her the bar bill was surprisingly modest. Just as well they had not found the champagne section of the wine list.

The party of four comprised Catherine, Alice, Nikolai and Bess. It became swiftly clear who could ski and who could not. While Nikolai and Alice were tearing down the slopes, executing the skiing equivalent of doughnuts and handbrake turns, Catherine traversed the blue piste at a sedate if controlled glide. Bess, legs fixed in snowplough position, could not have descended slower if she had been in a golf cart. While Bess shuffled about on the green slopes, Alice was swooping among the moguls like some tequila-fuelled Valkyrie.

But despite this devil may care approach, Alice had still remembered the most important piece of skiing equipment. A tube of sunblock. The combination of high-altitude, thin air and strong sunlight filtered through goggles is deceptive. By the time you feel that slight tingling of taut skin, the damage is done. And Alice, a girl capable of spending an hour in front of the bathroom mirror without a hint of irony or self-parody, knows this. Her morning preparations for the slopes consisted of foundation, moisturiser and goodness knows how many other balms, salves and unguents all applied in an unhurried ritual longer than the average Catholic Mass. And the difference from her sister could not be more pronounced. For Catherine, on the other hand, it is an infinitely more perfunctory and dismissive process.

In a temperate British summer, it makes no difference. But here, in the high mountains, you ignore skin care at your peril. Inevitably, by the end of the holiday, Alice looked as though she had just stepped off a catwalk while Catherine looked like a giant panda.

"Just say nothing" said Catherine when I picked her up from the station, exhibiting an uncharacteristic sense of humour failure. We spent much of the journey back home in silence, in the certain knowledge that even if I had been able to restrain myself, Catherine's brother was going to have a field day.

Alex saw the car draw onto the drive and met us at the front door. He greeted each sister with a big hug.

"Supper is ready. It's macaroni cheese" he said, then nodded at Catherine "although I expect you'd prefer bamboo shoots".


## 22 April 2012 – Dawn in Darlington

Standing bleary eyed in the pouring rain on Darlington station on a Saturday morning at seven was perhaps the principal downside of the trip, the hangover from a brilliant evening of fundraising but, by the same token, a night of no sleep . But there's nothing like a cold north-east morning to get the circulation pumping.

Let me back up a bit here. April 20th - The big nobs of the CPT were all MIA in Germany. Well specifically they were unavoidably detained in Tubingen on a critical bit of Eurobusiness. So Q asked me if I fancied going to Sedgefield for a fundraising dinner.

I was keen. No, really. Certainly keener than Q expected. Now, as you know, I am a Northern lad so I feel butterflies in my stomach when we pass Doncaster station, although that could have as much to do with the 'all day breakfast' sarnie I had needlessly subjected my constitution to at King's Cross. And I am positively misty eyed when we pass the plant works where, for a century, my ancestors built carriages and locomotives.

Q gave me the brief. The Institution of Mechanical Engineers North East Annual Dinner was to take place in Sedgefield (Mr Blair's former constituency for the more politically aware) and the engineers, bless their souls, have chosen to support Parkinson's research. My role was to bring a bit of CPT muscle to the local fundraising efforts, to help raise awareness of Parkinson's and to prise open wallets.

Our Man in Darlington was Simon, founder of Fix Parkinson's, unquestionably one of the rising stars on the fundraising circuit, and an engineer to boot. We first met last year, when I spoke at a local Parkinson's meeting, and hit it off immediately. It was good to pick up again where we left off. In fairness, considering Simon had been under the surgeon's knife only a fortnight earlier, he was surprisingly chipper. Bearing in mind that even a handshake from an orthopaedic surgeon can have lasting physical consequences, three hours of their tender mercies is not for the faint hearted. I still can't believe

Simon attended the dinner itself but he is made of strong stuff. What you or I might call 'excruciating pain' was waved away as a 'bit of discomfort'. By any standard, a canny lad.

The dinner itself was lots of fun. Inevitably in a male dominated field such as engineering, the dinner guests were predominantly men. I found myself on the top table, next to Scott, the chairman of the organisation. A bluff Glaswegian, we chatted at length about football, whisky and the Clyde shipbuilding industry. He delivered his speech and I did mine, before relaxing with a glass of Highland Park as the main after-dinner speaker strutted his stuff. The man in question was Robert Llewellyn, of Red Dwarf and Scrapheap Challenge fame. As an engineer manque, Llewellyn had the audience in stitches, recounting childhood welding experiments and so forth. Whatever happened to Mamod? And Meccano? But excellent though his talk was, I found it difficult to shake off the nagging feeling that someone was taking the wheels off my car at home. Or welding bits onto it. That's just how it is with engineers.

By the end of the evening, when all the money was counted, it came to just over three thousand pounds. In the midst of a recession, and in a part of the country hit particularly hard, this was breathtaking generosity. With support like this, you can believe we really will fix Parkinson's.

Top evening.

### 25 April 2012 – New bat

It's a bit of a macho thing among cricketers – who has the largest bat (yawn)? It probably goes back to the hunter-gatherer Cromagnon communities where the hominid with the largest club was best at killing sabre tooth tigers and therefore considered the best choice of mate.

And if you are one of those grunting Neanderthals who can wield a 2lb 12oz bat to good effect, all power to you. I am not and – let's face it – would probably have been eaten by the sabre tooths long ago.

Two seasons ago I was generously given a Black Cat Shadow, which tipped the scales at a brutish 2lb 11oz. It was magnificent – when you hit the ball, it stayed hit. But at the same time it kind of encouraged a more cavalier style of batting than my technique could sustain.

Last year, weakened by the Parkinson's, I used it less. Nothing wrong with the bat – when borrowed by others, this was still a monster bat. If bats were aeroplanes, this would be a B52. But by mid season, I was using a Kookaburra Blade which weighed a more manageable 2lb 8oz. I can't say that it improved my scores but it felt easier in the hand.

This year I have to face the fact that my old friend Mr Parkinson's has helped himself to more of my musculature and a lighter bat still is needed. I shall be a nurdler rather than a slogger so a fast manoeuvrable bat is the order of the day. And I think I have found it. A trip to Kent Cricket Direct led to an interesting solution. It needed to be light (I am no longer strong) and cheap (my ability level does not justify anything else). A chat with Paul and I have come away with a Chase Finback Harrow. And it makes sense. Lighter, easier and only marginally smaller. It also weighs only two pounds four ounces and before you say anything that's the same weight as Bradman's bat.

## 25 April 2012 – Away the lassies

7.26 am. Darlington to Kings Cross.

The train doors opened to shrieks and, as I climbed aboard, I had the distinct impression this could be a noisy journey. My principal concern catching such an early train from Darlington back to London, was that the train might be full of football fans on their way to some footballing Nirvana in the capital -- a train full of tribalism. In the event, the noise was coming not from Newcastle United fans but from something much more intimidating -- a party of secretaries from one of the local engineering firms on their way down to London for a hen night. Incidentally what is the collective noun for secretaries? Troop? Flange? Drove? School? Pod? I rather favour roost.

The roost heading down to The Smoke for the weekend were clearly bent on significant mischief. Each had removed engagement/wedding rings, applied warpaint with a trowel and adopted a false identity. 'Myrtle', 'Edna', 'Olive', 'Gladys' and 'Cynthia' were on the lash for the weekend and evidently planned to be awake for all of it. None had booked a hotel - there were enough clubs open all night to take care of the night hours. God help London.

The girls had boarded the train at Newcastle and it is fair to say that the roost were already in high spirits. The spirits in question being bottles of cherry sours. Each had a shot glass on a chain around their neck. In fact they had finished the first bottle before we reached Northallerton. At 7.43 am. By the time we pulled out of Doncaster, they had dismissed the sours and moved on to some sort of orange and chocolate liqueur that Gladys had found at the bottom of a cupboard in the kitchen and, despite the presence of chocolate, was not widely appreciated.

When we reached Peterborough, Myrtle, who had been quiet for a while, announced that she wasn't feeling very well. She was instantly frogmarched to the facilities by Olive who, if truth be told, didn't look too brilliant herself. Cynthia, holding her other arm, also looked a little the worse for wear, an appearance perhaps exacerbated by her unusual nail varnish. Applied somewhere between Newark and Peterborough, it was testament to the fact that you will never achieve a salon look if (a) you choose to apply the nail varnish whilst the train negotiates points at high speed and (b) you are pissed as a fart in the first place.

In fairness to the lasses, they kept us entertained for most of the journey. Cheerful drunks rather than morose or aggressive in that way men seem to drink. Judging by the way they all tumbled out of the train at King's Cross, I suspect it was probably a memorable weekend. Actually, probably the opposite because I doubt if any of them will remember a thing.

Incidentally Edna (just to clear up one thing for the record), although Grand Marnier contains orange, it does not count as part of your five a day.

# MAY

**5 May 2012 – Lover boy**

Adolescence can be a trying time for, well, adolescents. Whilst their bodies are growing and developing in all sorts of predictable and even unpredictable ways, their brains are perpetually stuck in first gear. It's rather like watching evolution in reverse gear. Even the most placid child becomes an acne riddled cross between a grunting Neanderthal man and a pit viper. And that's just the girls.

In many respects, the boys have it far worse -- it's difficult enough establishing any interest from the opposite sex at the best of times. But when you have a face like an overcooked pizza, you might as well familiarise yourself with the Saturday night TV schedules. Because, let's face it, you're not going out. Not now, not any time. Until your ever creative and changing physiology decides to pause for breath settles down a tad, and your neck and shoulders are less mediaevally septic, nights out are replaced by lights out. Say goodnight to the folks Gracie.

Such considerations are however purely human. Dogs are not bothered by such matters as physical appearance. To a dog, it matters not one jot whether the target of one's affections is a stunner or, well, a dog. Dogs have a -- how shall I put this -- rather robust interpretation of the word courtship.

Louis the poodle is eight months old. In canine terms, he is just entering the Kevin and Perry years. And in his mind, subjected to a maelstrom of unfamiliar hormones and neurotransmitters, everyone is available for some degree of, er, romantic interaction. Well, I say everyone but I mean everything. Animate or inanimate. Table legs and chairs are particular favourites and believe me, there is nothing more calculated to put you off your cornflakes than the sight of a poodle humping a chintz sofa. And when you shout "Louis!" at the top of your voice, he pauses only briefly to give you the kind of look that makes it clear that, in his estimation, the sofa had given him a clear "go" signal. She was asking for it.

It was the first time that I had ever thought of the sofa as female.

But even then, when you think that Louis cannot possibly embarrass you more, you discover that he has barely scratched the surface of his apparently limitless capacity. Such as last week when Wanda, mother of one of Alex's school friends dropped by to pick up a piece of jewellery. Even after many years of marriage, she was surprised by Louis's disproportionate interest in her. And persistence. And Louis certainly isn't one to indulge in extended foreplay.

Wanda is at least female. Not that these gender issues bother Louis. Called to a management meeting in Buckinghamshire last week at short notice, I was stuck for childcare. So I bundled Louis and Alex into the car with an explicit exhortation to be on their best behaviour, framed by a complex system of rewards and penalties involving McDonalds and tickets to the Lords Test.

Whilst this had an immediately salutary effect on Alex, its import was wholly lost on our poodle Casanova. Ten minutes after we arrived, I was called out of the meeting by a distracted Alex telling me that "Louis is bothering people". The sight of Louis shagging the leg of a man in a tweed suit was, unsurprisingly, my enduring image of the trip.

I sat in the car, head in my hands.

"Who was that man?" asked Alex.

"Chairman of the Trustees"

He winced.

"Not good, Dad".

"Not good, Alex".

## 14 May 2012 - The Blues and the Reds

In the end it came down to a goal deep in injury time to decide the 2012 premiership title. It really couldn't have been any closer, or left any later. After three thousand four hundred and twenty minutes of football, the champ and the contender were finally separated by a goal scored in the three thousand four hundred and twentieth minute. You really couldn't write this stuff.

For Manchester United this was particularly crushing. A season of what was, by their standards, promise but little achievement still looked like ending with the most significant piece of silverware English league football has to offer. Even as the game at Sunderland's ground (The Stadium of Light -- really, who dreams up these titles) ended, two minutes remained at Maine Road (or the Soup Bowl of Misery -- or whatever their home ground is called these days). Two minutes in which Manchester City ceased to be a team of habitual failures whose only purpose in life seemed to be to that of spectators to Manchester United's greater glory. In those two minutes, all the previous forty odd years were erased. Like those cheap cassettes that Beemer Bill used to sell from the boot of his aging BMW, a single play had completely erased all previous memories.

It also erased both QPR goals and even the moment when Joey Barton (such a puckish name for someone who, to all intents and purposes, is looking to maim anyone who enters the nominal exclusion zone around his feet) was sent off. If one entertained any lingering doubts as to whether they got the right man, the demonstration of classical Thai kickboxing on further members of the Man City team left nobody unmoved.

There is of course no greater rivalry in football than that between Manchester City and United. For as long as both teams have been in the premiership (or the first division, as people of my generation insist on calling it still), the fixtures have been the focus of each season. A chance to atone for previous failures. An opportunity to score legendary goals.

Perhaps the most memorable goal was scored in May 1974 by the iconic Denis Law. Law signed for Manchester United in 1962. When he left United in 1923 he had scored 237 goals for the club. Ironically, although for many years a Manchester United player, Law finished his career as a City player. And it was as a City player, in the 81st minute of the last game of the 1973-74 season, that he scored one of his most defining goals. A pass from the right gave him no time or space to control the ball. But, great striker that he was, he beat the keeper with a cheeky back heel, winning the game for City and, at the same time, relegating the opposition. Law walked away from the goalmouth without a celebration, his head down. The opposition that day? Manchester United.

## 16 May 2012 – Early one morning

3:58 AM: I glance over at the alarm clock which confirms my worst fears. My choices are straightforward -- I can stare at the ceiling for the next three hours until the rest of the family awakes. The gentle rumble of snoring throughout the house, like distant thunder, confirms that this will be a long wait. I half slip half slide my way out from under the covers, stubbing my toe on the bed end and tiptoe into the study as the first pickets of the dawn chorus strike up. The computer creaks into life. There are e-mails to answer. There always are. Today there is Gladys from Ripon who tells me that she enjoyed "Coming to Terms", the follow-up to "Slice of Life" and can't wait till the next one. October, Gladys. October.

I scribble down a few thoughts for the next blog and doze off in my chair.

5:21 AM: some sort of commotion in the garden jolts me awake like a slap across the face with a turbot. There is a large fox trying to get into the chicken coop. Although the mesh is as near as possible fox proof, the hens do not know this. For Blaise and Alice, two elderly rather dowager-like old birds, this is all too much for their constitutions. Fortunately, I release Louis into the garden to terminate this vulpine assault, just as Blaise is about to have an attack of the vapours. Basil Brush meanwhile clears our garden fence in one leap. No mean feat considering it is about the height of Beechers Brook. But he needn't have worried. Despite what I would've considered to be an unambiguous command, Louis's interpretation of "KILL!" and its accompanying semaphore gestures amounts to little more than a gentle amble to the centre of the lawn, a few tentative sniffs of the air and an extensive cocking of the leg over the early-season basil. Note to self: Pasta Al Pesto is off the menu tonight.

Although for the most part a relatively boisterous dog, you can always rely on Louis to show his sensitive side at exactly the wrong moment. Sniffing the air and urinating is not the response of a well-oiled killing machine.

6:00 AM the radio bursts into life. John Humphrys is busily toasting Tory MPs like crumpets over an open fire. Greece decides to hold another general election thus triggering the kind of sociopolitical upheaval associated with the 1917 Bolsheviks. Undeterred, the tabloids are whipping themselves into an onanistic frenzy over Joey Barton's tackle on the Manchester City striker and the possible censures that the Football Association might have at its disposal. The red tops discuss this rationally and at some length before concluding that, on the whole, public castration seems to be the people's choice.

6:22 AM: the sound of a dustbin lorry up the road reminds us that we have forgotten to put the bin out. And dustbinmen are far too busy to walk the five yards up the drive to collect the bin. No sirree. If your bin isn't positioned exactly on the perimeter of your property, a line as conceptually precise as the Greenwich Meridian, then the bin will not be emptied. And not only that. There will be a snotty note to the effect that this is your second warning and, faced with such recidivist behaviour, "further action may be taken". The message would probably have greater impact were it not written in blue crayon.

7:00 AM: my phone sounds a Prozac-cheery little ditty (which, although infinitely irritating, seems to be so deeply embedded in the phone's circuitry that I am at a loss to know how to change it). From the smorgasbord of medication available to me, I pick a Madopar, an Azilect, some propranolol, fat soluble vitamins and a couple of Neupro patches, washed down with a sip or two of mango juice. Who needs coffee.

7:11 AM: Claire and I between us issue the 11th "final" warning to the children that it is time to get up. Claire pulls on her boots and I quickly whisked her down the hill to the station, arriving back to find a furniture lorry blocking our drive while he delivers two sofas to the neighbours. My polite request to move the lorry is greeted with a sullen "why?" before his mate points out that this is my drive.

7:43 AM despite telling Alex for the last ten minutes that I am leaving "with or without you", he is still searching for cricket socks with one hand whilst eating peanut butter on toast with the other. A remarkable skill certainly. If only he could apply the same diligence and industry to his English homework. Species have become extinct in the time it take him to learn a Shakespeare sonnet.

By the time he is firmly ensconced in the car, the dustbin lorry is again across our drive, in essence blockading our drive. Although you might think that the revving engine and reversing lights would be a hint, the driver still refuses to move the lorry until he is good and ready. And just for a moment, anger wells and I find myself in agreement with tabloid justice.

7:58 AM haven't even had breakfast and already I have found myself in an argument, incited the dog to acts of unprecedented violence, and taken enough strong drugs to sedate the House of Lords.

Yesterday's milk curdles on my cornflakes. It's going to be that sort of day.

### 23 May 2012 – Rattus Norvegicus

I recognise the voice instantly even have not spoken in several months.

"What do you know about rats?" Andy asks, clearly eschewing the usual how-are-you-I'm-okay-and-the-family? small talk.

"Rats? As in small, scurrying rodents?" I ask

"The same" he says "what can I do with them?".

"Mmm" I ponder "don't casserole well".

"Be serious" he says "because I've got a bunch of the little buggers living under my shed".

This probably isn't the moment to tell him that 'bunch' is not the collective noun for rats. Or buggers.

For reasons that are largely historical, Andy has lodged in his head the notion that I am a world expert on small rodents. And whilst I can distinguish a rat from a squirrel, my knowledge of any pertinent facts about muridae fall short of the level of scholarship Andy evidently attributes to me.

In Britain there are essentially two types of rat -- Rattus Rattus and Rattus Norvegicus. For many of my readers, this will be about as far as they wish to travel. It's a rat -- who cares whether it learnt Latin. But bear with me. Rattus rattus, which appeared to have got its taxonomic name at a time when any word could be made to sound like Latin by adding the suffix 'us', is the black rat. And you might be forgiven for thinking that a black rat would be, well, black. But in actual fact they can be anything from light brown through to black. Usually with a paler underbelly. Originating in Southeast Asia, its principal claim to fame was to spread plague. Nice.

In Britain, although they can still be found, they have largely gone the way of the red squirrel, in this case being muscled out of the way by Rattus Norvegicus, a big brown bruiser of a rat, significantly larger, more aggressive and better adapted to urban environments. Your basic nightmare. In fact Rattus Norvegicus is the most successful social mammal on the planet after humans. Thank goodness they have never got the hang of Facebook. Even so, not many species of vermin are celebrated in the title of a rock album.

We only think of an infestation when we see rats by daylight. But of course rats are everywhere. It's often said that we are no more than ten feet away from a rat in any urban setting, a fact calculated to have girls gathering their skirts about them and squealing. In a manner not unlike rats, it has to be said.

I share this learning with Andy. A brief expletive laden soliloquy makes it clear that Andy is not looking to support a self-sustaining colony of rodents beneath his garden shed. His interest in rats extends as far as wanting to know the best means of getting rid of them.

It's clear too that Andy is not thinking of capturing them alive and rehabilitating them into it rodent society many miles away under false identities. Nor does he wish to take them alive for subsequent disposal. No, he wants them dead and he wants to see evidence of them being dead. So poison is out of the question. The last thing Andy wants is a family of large dying rodents expiring in some inaccessible reach beneath his garden shed just as the warm weather begins.

So our options essentially are rat traps -- the old-fashioned variety with a large metal bar to dispatch the said rodent. Andy inevitably has reached the same conclusion and merely wants my advice on how to tempt the rats into the traps. Because rats are notoriously suspicious, especially of anything new and shiny, they have to be coaxed into taking the bait. And although the conventional wisdom is that rodents like cheese, this is largely irrelevant. There are many more tasty morsels to a rat then cheese. And certainly many more effective baits.

To see the average sewer rat, is to see a fit animal (well as fit as anything can be that carries so many blood-borne diseases) well adapted to its environment. Rats are omnivores for certain, but they do have their preferences. Studies have shown that, when rats are provided with a cafeteria diet, essentially the average university student's food intake, they put on weight like crazy. When a rat is offered fruit as an alternative to the normal grain, he is happy to choose the fruit. But when it's a choice between fruit and chocolate digestives, the rats invariably ignore the healthy option. In fact they will go further, gnawing the chocolate off and leaving the rest of the biscuit.

Rats are fatally sweet toothed. Ask any professional ratcatcher. If you want to catch rats, you don't bait traps with ears of corn or breadcrumbs. No self-respecting rat is going to fall for that. On the other hand, marshmallows, peanut butter and condensed milk will bring them out better than the Pied Piper.

A brief inventory of the kitchen cupboards reveals an out of date bar of white chocolate. Perfect. We bait a trap, place it adjacent to the main runs and go indoors for a glass or two of Andy's homebrew. Incidentally rats love beer too. If you want to keep a rat happy (and I can't think why you would) then you can't do better than an egg cup full of bitter and the remains of last night's Pot Noodle.

An hour later, we pick up the torch and go looking for 'customers'. We have one already. And he is definitely a Norvegicus. Or, more accurately, was. Rather than deal with him now, we elect to leave him until daylight. I head home with Andy's undying thanks and several bottles of Old Throatwarmer.

The phone rings early the following morning. It is Andy. The dead rat has gone missing. Along with the trap. Andy is unimpressed. He now wants advice on how to deal with foxes.

There are of course thirty seven species of fox, the most common being the red fox *vulpes vulpes*....

### 31 May 2012 – Timezones

Like most Parkies, my life is dominated by pills and capsules. And by the tyranny of the clock -- the necessity to take the medicines at the times prescribed. Despite this I have an ambiguous relationship with time and the passage of time. Specifically, I don't wear a watch. It's not that I have anything against watches. More that all my timekeeping needs are amply addressed by my phone, car, computer, television and a host of other gadgets that are part of modern living. Even the microwave tells me the time, confidently playing its part in this digital conspiracy. No need for a portable timepiece.

Claire, on the other hand, is Clockgirl. At her behest, we have clocks - and old fashioned ones at that, with hands - in the living room, kitchen, bathroom and bedroom. The whole house ticks. At every verse end, I am reminded of the passage of time.

This wouldn't be so bad if the clocks were accurate. But each is between two and seven minutes fast.

There is, you may be surprised to read, nothing wrong with the mechanics of the clocks. Each is accurate to a second a month or whatever. No, the inaccuracy is imposed on these unsuspecting timepieces from, let me say, an outside agent in the form of my good lady wife.

Claire has the notion that this will assist punctuality. That by reacting to a clock that is five minutes fast, she will make the train, not miss it. These clocks will be the difference between sitting comfortably in carriage four of the 7:23 to Charing Cross and disconsolately watching its tail lights disappear in the morning mist. As if somehow, she has bought time.

Whilst the reasoning - and I cannot bring myself to say 'logic', aware that this is a hideous mangling of the word's true meaning - behind this is at least vaguely apparent, there seems to me to be a key flaw. Surely this cunning horological ruse can only hold sway if you are unaware of its imposition. In other words, you cannot surely be fooled by clocks that you have, yourself, deliberately set incorrectly.

But once again, I find I am wrong. Apparently you can. And when pressed on this point, Claire merely waves my argument aside. "That's just male logic" she says, cutting a swathe through deductive reasoning that would have left modern philosophy in tatters, and simultaneously leaving me openmouthed with an expression not dissimilar to a goldfish.

In fact the expression was exactly the same as the one I found myself wearing this morning when my mobile phone had somehow conspired to wake me at five. Since I was in Brussels, the bright little thing had decided, on a whim, to update itself to local time rather than British Summer Time. So instead of rousing me at six, as firmly instructed the previous evening, it took that to mean six, local time. Five, UK time. Not amused. In fact the very opposite of amused, as I jabbed at the off button, at the same time knocking a glass of water over.

My grandfather Tom, of choleric disposition, once hurled a still ringing alarm clock out of the bedroom window. Or more accurately through the bedroom window. He was not a man who much liked mornings. And beyond his enduring affection for the internal combustion engine in all its manifestations, not the kind of person who was much interested in machinery. Certainly not a man who had much truck with timepieces.

And at five, disorientated in a Brussels hotel, I knew exactly how he felt.

# JUNE

**5 June 2012 – Bells and bullies**

Thanks to my father's job as a GP in Yorkshire, I was afforded the benefit of a ludicrously expensive education in a Wiltshire boarding school. Hogwarts it was not, although some of the school buildings dated back to the 1740s. As, for that matter, did many of the geography department.

This education seems, with hindsight, to have served two useful purposes. Firstly it rid me of my Yorkshire accent, a change which still confuses people who do not know my roots. The genotype may be wholly Yorkshire but the phenotype is less geographically constrained, with vowels drawn, magpie-like, from the length and breadth of these sceptered isles. Most listeners cannot place me. Secondly, it introduced me to a group of friends who, although I see them less frequently (but immeasurably more cheerfully) than I see my dentist, have been a defining influence, a leitmotif, in my life.

If these were the useful outcomes of an education that cost a little over a hundred and eighty thousand pounds in today's money, one can draw a veil over the less valuable aspects. Careers advice, for instance, was comically inadequate. The output of the school went, in about equal numbers to Oxbridge, 'other universities' and the army. If you were good at biology, you were expected to be a doctor, while a propensity for English and history might indicate a future barrister. If you were Tim Nice-but-Dim, and many were, you need think no further than Sandhurst. I was good at French and German, a skillset so disappointingly alien to Doc Wright that he could offer nothing beyond a vague yawned "Well, there's always the foreign office I suppose", dismissing my aspirations in nine crushingly disinterested words. Naturally I chose to be a scientist.

At my school, bells began the day with (as if the smell of frying bacon and eggs were insufficient) a brief peal to signal breakfast and to rouse pupils from their beds. The school modelled itself on Oxbridge and its rituals. It even called itself 'college' and its headmaster 'master'. So single bells signified the passing of each lesson while persistent tolling marked times for individual prayer and collective worship. Sport, break and recreation times were punctuated by triple peals. And at the end of the day, a single strike called curfew and Mr Pettigrew would emerge from the porter's lodge, lantern in hand, to lock the gate to Court.

If it had been possible to have a bell to specify bowel movements, I'm sure the college would have found a way to integrate it into the timetable. Everything was regulated, controlled or in some way restricted. The college took the view that thirteen to eighteen-year-old boys were best kept occupied. In their jaded view of adolescence, free time equated to mischief.

They were of course correct. Nevertheless, since parents paid the equivalent in school fees of the Greek national debt, the college felt obliged to provide some sort of free time for their charges to relax, for young Tarquin to explore the creative potential of fire extinguishers, or for Piers to relieve the ennui of quadratic equations by duct taping the new boys to lampposts.

So when the evening end of prep bell sounded, your time was your own until curfew. About an hour and a half in which to do something productive, life enhancing or, if you were in the same house as Tarquin or Piers, try to avoid being subjected to one of their seemingly infinite repertoire of imaginative torture methods. It was the purest good fortune that this was the 1970s and therefore waterboarding had yet to be invented.

While the hours were marked by bells, the time between was marked by the malign presence of these two bullies prowling the corridors like Crabb and Goyle in search of prey. There was no limit to the humiliation this unholy pair would mete out to all those unfortunate enough to cross their paths. To its enduring shame, the college, resolutely blind or callously indifferent to their practices, did nothing, ascribing their reign of terror to youthful high jinks perhaps. When, in one Lent Term assembly, the master solemnly announced the untimely death of Tarquin during the holidays (killed, it later transpired, when he rolled the sports car he had stolen), he was shocked by the way in which the news was received. Suffice to say, there were few tears shed over this life cut short. Even Piers seemed strangely relieved.

Nobody likes a bully. Even other bullies.

I left the school in 1976 to become a scientist. Not a diplomat.

Piers was ordained in 1985 and became a missionary. And no, that isn't his real name. I owe him that.

## 9 June 2012 – Shirty!

Around October last year, I came up with a brilliant space-saving plan. I would pack all my summer clothes -- swimming trunks, shorts, T-shirts and Hawaiian shirts (I've only got one) -- into a suitcase. The same suitcase would then go in the loft, thus liberating my limited cupboard space (I am male and therefore, in this household, allocated only such clothing space as is absolutely necessary without encroaching on frock space) for my equally numerous Arran and Fair Isle sweaters.

Brilliant, yes?

There is however one tiny picosnag in all of this. It is imperative -- and I mean imperative -- to ensure that the suitcase chosen as repository for one's summer wardrobe is not the same suitcase chosen by good lady wife for dispatch of unwanted garments to the charity shop. It's important to check.

Needless to say, I didn't.

Of course the consequences of this lapse should have become apparent earlier. Indeed they would have become apparent earlier had there been anything approximating a summer to speak of. So we are now well into June and it is only now that the sequence of events and their consequences have become manifest.

So my entire summer wardrobe found its way to a charity shop somewhere in Tonbridge last October. This is, by any standards, a significant failure in marital communication. It also probably speaks volumes about my questionable sartorial leanings that nobody in the household batted an eyelid at the prospect of the whole job lot going to charity. Okay it may not be the Dolce and Gabbana Spring collection, but surely they weren't that shabby. I had been wearing his clothes only days earlier. Some were new.

Still, my loss is Tonbridge's gain. And these events go a long way towards explaining the unsettling feeling I've had for several days, that half of the town seems to be wearing my clothes. They are. And the worst part of it all? The clothes look better on them than they do on me.

## 11 June 2012 – The beautiful game

Anyone of a certain age who grew up in the tribalistic shadow of the 1966 World Cup, supported a football club. It was simply a part of growing up. If you were a Londoner, it might be West Ham, with their claret and blue shirts, led by Bobby Moore, the last gentleman footballer. If you were unfortunate enough to be born west of the Pennines you probably become misty eyed over Busby's Babes (a moniker, incidentally, which still makes me think of top shelf magazines more than footballers). But if, like me, you grew up in God's Country, your footballing allegiances had only one legitimate outlet, at Elland Road, home of the pride of Yorkshire, Leeds United.

Being in my mid-50s, the Leeds United that I remember was the iconic side of Don Revie. To this day, in the same way that Catholics can recite the Hail Mary, I can remember the details of that mighty team -- Gary Sprake, Paul Reaney, Paul Madeley, Billy Bremner, Jack Charlton, Norman Hunter, Peter Lorimer, Allan Clarke, Mick Jones, Johnny Giles and Eddie Gray.

Gary Sprake, a mixture of inspiration and exasperation in goal, was capable of pulling off acrobatic saves of almost balletic beauty and then, from nowhere, gifting the opposition a goal in circumstances that invariably find their way into "what happens next?" compilations. Such as the memorable moment in 1967 when he somehow contrived to hurl the ball into his own net at Anfield. For the rest of the afternoon, the cops treated him to an unending chorus of Des O'Connor's Careless Hands. It remains one of life's injustices that he is remembered more for the tiny handful of occasions he cost Leeds a game than the huge majority where he saved the game.

In front of Sprake were the Pauls -- Reaney and Madeley -- two of the finest, yet least celebrated, full-backs in the league at that time. In any other club but Leeds, with its array of talent, they would have been justly feted for their miserly goal allowances. Paul Reaney, the right back, was almost always looking to overlap the midfield, in essence the game's first wingback, although there was no such term in those no-nonsense days at Elland Road. And at the same time, he was acknowledged even by George Best to be one of the finest man-to-man markers in the game.

Paul Madeley could and often did play anywhere on the field. Although nominally a full-back he was comfortable even as a winger. During his time at Leeds he wore all the shirts from number two to eleven and, you have to remember, this was back in the days when shirt numbers related to position rather than squad numbers. His retirement, a time for reflection on the many glories of the time, has been dogged by ill-health -- a brain tumour in 1992, a heart attack in 2002 and, as if this were not enough, he was diagnosed with Parkinson's in 2003.

The Leeds midfield trio of Bremner, Charlton and Hunter were the powerhouse of Revie's dreams. Billy Bremner, the human embodiment of a fox terrier, never gave up on any ball, never stopped running and harassing opposition players. And when he had hounded an opponent into releasing possession, he would distribute the ball quickly and effectively, usually to Johnny Giles.

In the same way that Bremner controlled the ground, snapping at opponents' heels, Jack Charlton commanded the air. Supremely tall and imposing, Jack was more than a match for any centre forward, even "our kid" as he affectionately described his brother Bobby who just happened to play for a team on the other side of the Pennines.

But wearing the number six shirt was the man who, more than any other, embodied the physical -- even, dare one say, cynical -- type of football that defined Leeds United in the early 1970s. If Bremner was a terrier,

Norman Hunter was a Rottweiler. Hunter had no illusions about his role. The ball might get past him sometimes. Or the player might. But on no occasion would both pass him. And yet, whenever he was booked or sent off for brutally scything an opponent down, as he so often was, Norman somehow managed to feign a hangdog expression of innocence worthy of Shakespearean theatre. When the Leeds trainer was once told that Hunter had broken a leg, his reaction was "whose?"

On the right-wing was Peter Lorimer, the youngest player ever to take the field for Leeds, making his debut at fifteen. A Scot with a cannon of a right foot, there was no more terrifying sight for a goalkeeper than Lorimer lining up a free kick. Capable of scoring from thirty yards out, pity the poor souls who had to form part of the wall. More than once Lorimer concussed players with direct hits. To my recollection, only one goalkeeper ever saved a Lorimer penalty, and that was at the expense of a broken wrist.

To his immediate left was Allan "Sniffer" Clarke. In a largely homegrown team (difficult to grasp in this age of highly paid mercenaries, but this was the norm then), Sniffer joined the club from Leicester City in 1969, immediately justifying Revie's faith in him with twenty six goals in his first season. A stylish dribbler, he had that knack, like all the best strikers, of being in the right place at the right time. If Bremner and Hunter were rough purposeful earthenware, Clarke was fine bone china.

And Clarke could have no better foil than the Leeds centre forward Mick Jones, a strong, courageous old-fashioned work horse of a target man. His muscular energy in the middle created the havoc in opposition defences upon which Clarke thrived. I still remember him collecting his 1972 FA Cup winner's medal, arm in a makeshift sling, his face contorted with pain from a dislocated elbow suffered in the last minute

In the number ten shirt was Johnny Giles, a genial, soft-spoken leprechaun of infinite subtlety and touch, a foil to Lorimer's sabre. Along with Bremner, Giles controlled the game. Bremner won the ball and Giles would distribute the fruits of that victory. If Michelangelo had been reincarnated in as a footballer, it would have been as Johnny Giles.

Completing this glittering side was Eddie "The Last Waltz" Gray. A classic winger, in many ways a throwback to a former era of football, the twinkle-toed Gray would ghost past defenders before cutting inside to shoot or lashing in crosses for Mick Jones or Big Jack. In a team built on the muscular ball winning of Bremer and Hunter, no player better embodied the finesse to which Leeds aspired. Amazingly, in side that attracted cards like bees round a hive, Gray was never booked.

Don Revie's Leeds were a Jekyll and Hyde enigma. Playing in an all white strip, an aspirational nod to Real Madrid and their fancy continental football, they somehow never quite achieved what their talents deserved. So often the bridesmaid, rarely the bride.

Never a popular side, Leeds were often demonised by the predominantly southern press for a brand of football that was seen as cynical. Certainly Leeds played a style of football that was, by any standards, physical and aggressive, but it was rarely as calculating as portrayed. And the media emphasis on the decisive, even brutal, tackling of the Leeds defenders somehow shone the spotlight away from the luminous creativity of the Leeds midfield and poetic expression of the strikers.

Even at their worst, they were a difficult side to beat. But at their best, Leeds played champagne football, posturing and preening like matadors. And for nearly a decade, Don Revie's men were the footballing manifestation of Yorkshire -- that unique combination of coal-fired grit and determination, with the poetry and lyricism of the North York Moors.

When, in 1971, I went away to boarding school, I found myself alone among southerners. Among so many who supported Arsenal, Chelsea, West Ham and Spurs, I was the only boy from Yorkshire there. It marked me out.

"So who do you support?" they would ask, in plummy Home Counties accents.

"I support Leeds United" I said.

And I was proud.

## 17 June 2012 – Cricket as a metaphor for life

It's a long story but, for a variety of reasons I found myself umpiring rather than playing today. And it's fair to say that you see the best and the worst of human nature from the umpire's viewpoint.

We were playing another Sussex village club's 4th XI and, for the most part, we were well-matched. They, like us, had a mixture of wide-eyed youngsters and those in the, er, twilight of their cricketing careers. Their captain, John, a wise old bird, was charming and entertaining.

In the absence of suitable others, I volunteered to umpire. As a way to lose friends and annoy people, umpiring is, of course, without parallel. When did you last give a batsman out only for the player to congratulate you on your eagle-eyed, split second decision making? Precisely. Never.

Early on in the opposition's innings, I had occasion to give an opposition batsman out LBW, a decision I took with a little more certainty than perhaps I would or should, with hindsight. The keeper told me afterwards that the ball was heading for the stumps although, looking back, height was possibly an issue and he was rather more forward than I initially thought. Still, the Bayham bounce (or lack thereof) has to be factored in.

It was probably one that would have been reviewed if I am honest. But, beyond a little grumpiness, that should have been that. It mattered not whether it was the correct decision or not, he was still out. Why? He was out because he was given out.

But what followed was shameful. A long, Wayne Rooneyesque vocal tirade as he walked back to the pavilion was directed toward me and anyone who would listen, despite his fellow batsman's attempts to make him be quiet. Once he had gone, his fellow bat apologised profusely, embarrassed by this outburst. His captain, next in, was equally apologetic, aware that, whatever the provocation, this behaviour had not so much crossed a line but erased it.

Nobody likes being given out when they feel themselves wronged. But most handle that disappointment with dignity, knowing perhaps that one day the umpire may give them a life they didn't deserve. It all evens up and the older players have the dignity and maturity to accept that. They do not presume to lecture the umpire.

But that sadly is the spotty, whining arrogance of youth. His fellow opener was embarrassed by his behaviour. His captain was embarrassed by his behaviour. Only he was not.

Well listen up sonny. Life isn't always fair. Some days bad things happen and mummy can't always make it better. You got given out. I got Parkinson's in my 40s. Neither of us got the 'decision' we wanted. You will at least get another innings.

Life can be a bitch. Get over it.

Oh, and grow up a bit, eh?

## 18 June 2012 – What I need

I can't imagine the postbag this will incur from angry readers but I'll say it anyway – I think Father's Day is an invention of the card manufacturers. There I did it... hate me!

Mother's Day is associated with Mothering Sunday, a Christian festival and is celebrated on the fourth Sunday in Lent. Father's Day falls on the feast of St Clinton of Hallmark.

OK I made the last bit up. In actual fact, Father's Day can be traced to a woman in the US with the magnificent name of Sonora Smart Dodd (1882-1978), who in 1910, being pretty fond of her dad, called for a day to celebrate fathers.

Her father was not a greetings card manufacturer. Definitely not. Never. No sirree.

## 27 June 2012 – 'Delete as appropriate' blues

I like most music. Well, apart from hip-hop, rap or any of those forms of music which seem to be shared on a Saturday night from small lime green hatchbacks with speakers the size of refrigerators.

I like classical music, opera, progressive rock, you name it. But among all this, I have a particular fondness for the blues. If I had ever been a musician, I think I would have liked to be a blues musician.

Years of extensive research -- well I've listened to a few records -- lead me to conclude that there are essentially four critical components to being a successful blues man.

(1) The music. That's a doddle -- you just need a guitar, the older the better. It probably doesn't even matter too much if the tuning is a bit wonky. That seems to me to be part of the charm. But it needs to be an acoustic guitar really. Those rock axes just don't work here. Remember, you're aiming for a sort of wooden porch front in the evening twangy sort of sound. If you can rope in one of those American midwest Prairie train whistles, then you're halfway there. Then pick three chords and learn them. How difficult can it be?

(2) The voice. This one's a little bit trickier and you may want to start early. I'm not talking about years of vocal training, swooping scales, fancy trilld and arpeggios. Quite the opposite. Pretty much all the blues musicians have voices that sound as though they gargle with battery acid. Maybe they do. But on the whole, this kind of gravelly rasp takes a couple of decades of voice abuse before that vocal patina is perfected. It's not easy to short-circuit this process but if you're determined to try, then I recommend

you familiarise yourself with Rebel Yell, a liquid that eats through polished furniture for goodness sake. Imagine what it can do to vocal cords. Despite its corrosive properties, it is amazingly marketed as a bourbon. Keith Richards drinks Rebel Yell. Enough said.

(3) The name. This one is critical. If you get nothing else right, don't get this wrong. If your name isn't already a kosher blues name, like John Lee Hooker, change it. Sometimes you have no option. McKinley Morganfield would never have made it -- but Muddy Waters, his chosen blues name, guaranteed success. The earnestly named Chester Arthur Burnett has a whiff of chartered accountancy no matter how well he sang. But Howlin' Wolf shipped records by the lorry load. Same man. And, let's face it, Henry Roeland Byrd is not a patch on Professor Longhair.

If you're really stuck, just pick the place where you live. Lizzie Douglas became Memphis Minnie for instance while John Smith Hurt became Mississippi John to good effect. Of course this works better if you live in one of those states south of the Mason Dixon line. The fact that there is no Spaghetti Junction Mike, Halifax Harry or Droitwich Derek is testament to the fact that the above only applies to America. But then so does blues.

Of course places are only one approach. Dietary preferences worked well for Antoine 'Fats' Domino and Aaron Thibeaux 'T-bone' Walker. Gastrointestinal ailments were the road to riches for Huddie William 'Leadbelly' Leadbetter. But for me, the award for the best blues name ever has to go to Deacon Bates, or as he is better known, Blind Lemon Jefferson.

So the rules seem to be places, favourite foods/drinks, ailments and handicaps.

I can't pick between Jonny "Sauternes" Stamford or Jonny "Tremor dominant Parkinson's" Stamford. I'll get back to you.

(4) The words. I've got this one buttoned down. Essentially all blues songs follow a strict formula -- the singer has woken up in the morning and some major life event has either taken place or is about to take place and, on the whole, their morning is not panning out exactly according to plan. Oh, and the dog is dead. Usually. Or run away.

Of course most blues songs are more than fifty years old so they probably need updating. Something like this:

"DELETE AS APPROPRIATE BLUES"
by
Jonny "Tremor dominant Parkinson's" Stamford

*Well I woke up this morning*
*My* [wife/dog/best friend/civil partner] *wasn't there*
[He/she/it] *left me* [for another man/for another dog/a full English breakfast]
*The bed was* [cold and lonely/covered in labrador hair/a Slumberland Posturepedic]
*I poured myself a* [whisky/coffee/skinny latte]
*I* [got so mad/was really decidedly irritated]
*I fetched my* [gun/staple gun/Telegraph crossword]
*I got in my* [old Chevy pickup/practical Fiat Multipla/safety conscious Volvo S80]

*I drove* [real crazy fast/quite fast but always paying attention to fuel consumption/strictly within the speed limit and in the correct lane].
*and went and shot* [my cheating wife/a round of 68]
*Oh I got dem old* [lovesick/carsick] *blues*

# JULY

## 4 July 2012 – Getting at my meds

I'm beginning to think that this is a conspiracy. A conspiracy to make life difficult for those of a Parky persuasion such as myself.

Let me explain.

Each day I take a cornucopia of medicines, vitamins and what, in the Victorian vernacular, might be called 'tonics'. Some, such as levodopa, benserazide, rasagiline, rotigotine and propranolol, are prescribed by my neurologist. Others are 'prescribed' by myself, on what I have to confess are not always the most evidenced-based of grounds. These typically include multivitamins (well I don't always eat sensibly), high doses of vitamin E (fat soluble antioxidants seem like a good idea anyway), gingko biloba (strange Japanese stuff that thins the blood so you have to be a bit cautious with this one), and omega-3 fish oils (hardly any evidence base for this at all – I only take it as it might preserve my intellect for longer. And my brain is, as Woody Allen would say, my second favourite organ). I would take Q10 if I could afford it without having to sell my car, and it was available in proper pharmaceutical grade preparations rather than the footling little conscience-assuaging happy pills available from the health food shops.

Q10 or no Q10, it's a lot of pills, capsules, tablets, patches, and caplets. Incidentally what is a caplet? Something is either a capsule or tablet surely. Not some halfway house in between. The same with Jaffa cakes -- they're either a cake or a biscuit. And even more incidentally, I have decided unilaterally that they are cakes. No buts. They're cakes. Move on.

Back to the tabsules or whatever they're called. Like all Parkies, the tyranny of the tablets marks our every day. Our lives are punctuated by beeps, pings, trills and warbles, as each alarm signals another dose of something or other to stop us shaking, freezing, quivering or wobbling. But despite the ridiculous quantity of different pills, it's not they that invoke my wrath.

It's the packaging. I defy anybody with normal dexterity to extract a ten milligram propranolol tablet from its blister pack easily. To give you an insight into Parky World, imagine doing the same task wearing two layers of surgical gloves. Not so darned easy, huh? Yet that is, in functional terms, the task that I'm expected to perform at 7 AM each morning, with the dopamine tank running on empty. Not surprising then that these microscopic pink tablets either doggedly refuse to leave their blisters or tumble out in gay abandon. And when the little blighters escape, they are so small as to be practically invisible. Eventually they turn up, long after I have ceased looking for them. In the last three months alone, I have found the tablets among my socks, in my cornflakes, in the dog's fur and, on one particularly puzzling occasion, on the inside of my left nostril.

But blister backs are no better and no worse than the standard childproof bottle caps. Childproof they may be but they are also Parky proof. To open them, you have to press down on the lid with the kind of force associated with the gravitational pull of large planets. Or you must squeeze the lid with the pincers of a giant Guam coconut crab. And there's nothing that quite equals the sense of rising anxiety one experiences as one starts to go 'off' while wrestling with the lid of the Madopar bottle. You Parkies know what I'm talking about. How many times have you reached for the hammer.... Okay, but I bet you thought about it.

I have a dosette box and my Sunday evening ritual consists of filling the compartments with the many varied Smarties that keep me alive for another week – the medicines that make the difference between a dribbling, uncontrollably quaking version of me, unable to walk (that you don't see) and the near normal, slightly slow, cricket-loving Jon (that you do). So yes, I'm grateful for my medicines. But is it too much to ask that I should be able to get at the blessed things without a wrestling match.

Please.

Pretty please.

## 11 July 2012 – Olympic Fever

Rather than elicit a Batemanesque response of collective national incredulity, I'll just whisper it. Just between you and me, I'm not actually that fussed about the Olympics. Yes, that's right -- I don't mind who wins or loses. Is that terribly unpatriotic?

I shan't lose sleep over personal quests and personal bests, I will probably sleep through most of the events, especially the longer ones, and certainly the more slow paced and the least televisual. I can't see myself paying anxious attention to the medal leaderboard either.

As far as I'm concerned, it's an unfocused sprawling mass of endeavour and, whilst I respect and applaud the athletes in their fields, I'm afraid I have no great interest in actually watching them. Most of the events bear little relation to the classical Olympiad anyway. The original Olympic games reflected essentially military disciplines and I can grudgingly see the logic in that. Spear hurling and rock throwing becoming the javelin and shot put respectively, while rowing and sailing became -- well -- rowing and sailing. But essentially they were all martial skills. In the same way that Soviet tanks and missiles would parade through Red Square, the Olympic Games were meant to parade and display the strength of the military. The games were essentially about running, throwing, hitting and pulling. Pretty much basic training fare at Sandhurst to this day.

The same cannot be said of beach volleyball. It's hard to imagine this particular discipline giving any Spartan admiral cause to rethink his invasion plans. Equally, I don't see Hannibal and the Carthaginians turning to ping-pong tables as he made his way through the Alps. "No thank you, I'll stick with the elephants, if it's all the same." And as for synchronised swimming, enough said. I mean why? Just why?

Londoners, of course, will be exposed to several new sports during the 2012 Olympiad. Such as the 5000m frantic rush with briefcase as one discovers that athletes get preferential use of the tubes and one is forced to walk. Or run. Or the claustrophobia crush in which one stands nose to nose with a group of Turkish holidaymakers in the blazing heat of a London bus heading from Pimlico to Walthamstow during rush hour.

I suggest there is too much emphasis on athleticism -- if I was Prime Minister, we would have altogether more genteel sport. The cross-country stroll, the 200 metre amble and the not-terribly-long jump. And who would wish to sprint when you could saunter, or run when you could dawdle.

You know, I think you could make a strong case for the egg and spoon race.

## 13 July 2012 - The observatory

One huge asset of my school, both literally and figuratively, was a magnificent telescope, donated by the Radcliffe Society in 1934 and housed in a green domed observatory at the top of the playing fields. Having developed, from nowhere I can remember, a strong interest in astronomy in my early teens, I was nearly always to be found there. After prep each evening, if the skies were clear and dark, I'd head for the observatory.

From the college gates, with the chapel on your left and the "Bridge of sighs" on your right, you passed the last street lamp in the car park behind the all-weather pitch and headed up through the gate onto the playing fields. From there you were in pitch darkness until, as your eyes adjusted, you could vaguely make out the shapes of trees. On the left, perhaps two hundred yards away, the tell-tale red pinprick glow of cigarettes could be seen in the bushes that marked the perimeter of the beagle kennels.

After some four hundred yards of dead reckoning, you passed a clump of ancient hornbeams, and a flutter of wings from Bader, an aged but vocal tawny owl. The path turned North West for a further two hundred yards past the brooding gothic silhouette of the cricket pavilion, at which point the dome of the observatory could just be picked out against the skyline. Sometimes a faint red glow from one of the windows would provide a beacon, at the same time telling you that someone was already there and would, in all probability, have already put the kettle on.

Of course, clear nights meant frozen fingers thrust deep in pockets and brisk energetic walking, your breath billowing in front of you. Cold enough for chilblains. Although the fashion was for pupils to wear their jackets unbuttoned in adolescent defiance, we wore ex-military greatcoats, scarves and gloves. On still nights your clumping booted feet crunched the frost, weaving tracks across the fields. Inquisitive hedgehogs followed, looking for insects in your footsteps. In the moonlight between scudding clouds, sometimes foxes would play with their cubs on the open fields below the observatory.

Sometimes we would turn the mighty telescope on the deepest recesses of the universe, barely glimpsed galaxies hundreds of millions of light years away in the constellation of Virgo, each made up of a hundred thousan million stars like our own. Or we would be dazzled by the Pleiades, clusters of stars on our celestial doorstep. It mattered not. Every time one changed the field of view, some new wonder would appear -- nebulae, globular clusters, spiral galaxies and gas clouds on the belt of Orion. I've looked on, like Perseus the hunter, as fireballs passed through the great constellation of Andromeda, lighting the skyline as they went. I've seen things people wouldn't believe.

Sometimes we would look at Saturn and its rings, Jupiter and its moons circling like bees, or the eerie green light from Neptune, at the edge of our solar system. Occasionally we would wrap ourselves in our greatcoats and recline in deckchairs to watch meteor showers, squealing with delight as each bright shooting star crisscrossed the heavens. And I will never forget my first comet. Comet West, visible in the early hours of the summer of 1975, its tail projecting away from the sun, blown on the solar wind.

We all claimed to be scientists, recording our observations in meticulous detail and charting planetary courses and lunar occultations. But for me it was much more that. It was freedom from the tyranny of college, its structure and order. It was a bunch of friends I still see today, older and wiser certainly, less frequently of course. But friends, close friends, nonetheless. If the school gave me little else, these alone were gifts enough.

To some extent we took it all for granted. A telescope in its own observatory is an astonishing thing for teenagers. For the five years I was at the school, I had access to nearly professional telescopic facilities. And all so that the boys could gaze at stars.

But it was more than all that. For me there was something absolutely primal about staring at stars on cold clear nights. Knowing that the light from these stars had taken centuries, millennia and more to reach me. And wondering if, somewhere out in that glittering void, there was life. Above all, it was the sense of staring into eternity.

### 17 July 2012 – A lesson in organisation

The Duke of Edinburgh award scheme was founded in 1956 by the nation's favourite Greek gaffe merchant to give young people the chance to develop skills for work and life, fulfil their potential and have a brighter future (it says here). The award has three levels -- bronze, silver and, you've guessed it, gold. Bronze, essentially the entry-level, has four sections -- volunteering, physical, skills and expedition. Within each category but the last, there is much flexibility in what activities you might choose.

But perhaps the most arduous, and certainly the most prescriptive, part of the DoE is the expedition. In this the examinees are expected to navigate, over the course of two days and a night spent under canvas, from point A to point B on the map. These points are around twenty miles apart and, to complete the task successfully, require the use of a compass and map. There are a number of checkpoints on the way. And of course you have to put up a tent. And also cook your own food -- always a challenge for the boys. Okay, it's not the North face of The Eiger, but it still constitutes a fair physical if not intellectual challenge for this TV remote generation. You are expected to complete the task without recourse to gadgetry. Or, and each year the headmaster feels the need to reiterate this, public transport. Mobile phones are expressly prohibited, as are GPS devices. Satnav is an absolute no no. In any case, mobile phones are pointless as the pupils have found to their cost that the local Domino's is under strict orders from the headmaster not to deliver pizza to any address that consists solely of an ordnance survey map reference.

Still, given halfway decent weather, the task is not overly challenging to the navigational skills of the average 15-year-old boy. Or so I thought last week. I had my verbal instructions from Alex. On Wednesday morning, I was to drive him to Leigh green, the start point -- in other words the village green in Leigh, a small conurbation five miles to the west of Tonbridge, in Kent, where his expedition team was to assemble.

There are two key points here. The instructions were verbal and – bit of local knowledge here - Leigh is pronounced as in the untruth 'lie'. These are important points.

Wednesday dawned and Alex, having not made the necessary arrangements himself, and having lost the original letter from the school giving the details of the assembly point, phoned a friend for details of the meeting place. Leigh green he was reminded. Of course Alex's adolescent interlocutor did not think to spell Leigh (why would you?) and Alex, who had never heard of the place anyway, wrote it down phonetically as 'Lie Green' and set about locating this on the map. In an effort to put paid to his reputation for disorganisation, so richly deserved in this family, and aware that I had an important teleconference immediately following drop-off, he pressed the coordinates into the satnav.

"Ah, this Lye Green" I said as we finally arrived in, a small Sussex hamlet just north of Crowborough, some ten miles to the south of Tunbridge Wells (i.e. emphatically not five miles to the west of Tonbridge). Alex looked confused. "Not Leigh green then? As in L-E-I-G-H?" I asked,

It was apparent that we were alone. There was no sign of boys with backpacks and tents. Nor anybody much. If this had been a Western, there would have been tumbleweed. And Lee Van Cleef with a pocket watch. Moreover, there was no obvious meeting point in this tiny little hamlet. Several enquiries and examination of possible rendezvous points, including a shrub nursery and a surprisingly large Baptist Church, failed to unearth the remaining members of Alex's team. I suggested, with my usual tact, that there might have been a tiny little mixup over the meeting point that he might perhaps like to resolve as a matter of urgency. Needless to say, I expressed this in far fewer words and rather more directly than I have done here. The phrase "get your life together" may even have crossed my lips.

A couple of uncomfortable calls to the school -- he was delaying the entire trip from departing -- established the source of the misunderstanding. It would take us nearly half an hour to reach Leigh, by which time the team would have to be well underway. Needless to say, I used much of that half-hour to explain to Alex the consequences of his geographical inexactitude for his pocket money expectations and a range of eagerly anticipated summer treats. A brief but contrite -- on my part – apology and discussion with the DoE assessor reached a compromise. We would drive instead to Penshurst and he would intercept his team there without penalty to himself or to his team.

We waited thirty minutes in Penshurst, sheltering in the church porch in driving rain, a half hour I used to hammer home my take on Alex's personal likelihood of *"the chance to develop skills for work and life, fulfil his potential and have a brighter future"*.

I was fuming. What is it about teenage boys? I'm not letting any cat out of the bag when I say that they are pathologically disorganised, capable of conjuring chaos from order, and elevating brinkmanship to an art form. Or is it just my son? On a test of geographical abilities, independent thinking and organisation, it takes an egregiously scrambled intellect to fail even to reach the correct start line. It's rather akin to Michael Schumacher failing to start a race because he was stuck in traffic. Or the Queen skipping a royal garden party because she had double booked with a whist drive. Or British Airways cancelling flights because they had forgotten to buy enough aeroplanes.

By the time I joined the teleconference, three quarters of an hour late, the chairman was winding up proceedings. I apologised for my tardiness, to widespread if weary amusement.

"You know, Jon" said the chairman laughing "you are just so disorganised! You need to get your life together."

## 22 July 2012 - Hifi heaven

I've always been into music -- in the sense of listening to music rather than playing I regret to say. I never learnt an instrument, but that's another story. Much of this love of music was inculcated at school in the 1970s where I was surrounded by music of all sorts. Well, rock if you were 'cool' or classical, if you're the kind of person who buttoned their sports jacket and wore NHS glasses held together by zinc oxide plasters.

But more than the music, the fascination of the time was hi-fi, then to a large extent in its infancy. Of course the definition of hi-fi (high fidelity) bore little relation to the practicalities. At my school, people less interested in the accuracy of the sound reproduction than in its power and bass. And here size was everything. Nobody cared much about your tweeters, but if you had ten inch woofers, you were accorded serious respect. And if you listened to Emerson, Lake and Palmer on said woofers, you were antarctically cool.

I wasn't. I had a cheap little cassette player with a handful of tapes, none of them cool, or even tepid. While the cool school were listening to Yes, the Doors Hawkwind, Jimi Hendrix and Santana, I was still enjoying Wings. I'm blushing as I write this.

But I was also beginning to listen to classical music. In my final year at school, I was billeted with one of the music teachers and his family. And the house echoed to the sound of music. Bob played the French horn, Sue was an oboeist. Not surprisingly their children were also accomplished musicians. Living there for a year was a revelation. I was introduced to the music of Elgar, Delius,

Bruckner and Mahler. Amazing sound worlds I could not have imagined. I even met composers, who would drop by the house when in the area. Also, and I can admit this nearly forty years later, I had a bit of a crush on Bob's daughters.

When I was young, not quite twenty I guess, I bought my first hi-fi setup from my very first pay packet. Or more accurately from my first three pay packets. I remember it very clearly: a Pioneer PL 514 turntable, JVC J-AS11G amplifier and Wharfedale Glendale XP2 speakers. To this I later added a Hitachi 220 cassette deck and a J-TV11G tuner.

It cost around three hundred pounds, a sum which amounted to 3 weekly pay packets but which, with the fiscally relaxed nonchalance of youth, I deemed to be particularly good value. Certainly the hi-fi magazines considered this to be a "budget" setup.

A decade later, my musical tastes had changed and I was more demanding when it came to hi-fi. Out went the Pioneer, JVC and Wharfedales to be replaced by a Dual 505, NAD 3130 and a pair of B&W DM 220 speakers. More clarity, more detail and more precision. That was in 1985.

And it was also the occasion when my ears were again opened. I had heard the early CD players and was keen to own one. So after extensive research I found the model I was looking for and tripped down to a small shop in the Charing Cross Road where my chosen CD player was for sale.

The ground floor of the shop sold CDs. In the basement was another low ceilinged room full of hi-fi. To one side, separated by a sliding glass screen, was a listening room.

As I went through the process of purchasing my CD player, the listening room was prepared for another client. Initially I paid no attention, focused entirely on my own purchase. But as the opening brass chorale from Mahler's third Symphony rang out, I found myself drawn in. The sound, even through the glass screen, was breathtaking in its clarity and power. It was, and is oft said, as though one was actually present at the recording. Such was the presence.

I looked into the room. The sound appeared to be emanating from two large radiators. Even with my modest knowledge of hi-fi, and plumbing for that matter, I realised that they must be speakers of some sort. I asked the assistant.

"You can't afford them" he said with a laugh.

"I'm sure you're right" I said "but what are they?"

"They are Quad electrostatics".

"Purely out of interest" I asked, with what I saw as an overdose of nonchalance, "how much do they cost?"

The shop assistant advised me to sit down. He was right to. The speakers in question were for sale at three thousand six hundred pounds a pair. Even today that is a jawdropping sum of money for a pair of speakers. In 1985 it was almost unimaginably expensive. The cost of a significant car. But then of course they were most of the size of a car.

I listened for a good half an hour, overwhelmed by the presence of these speakers. And walking home, even with my new CD player, I could think of little else but what I had heard and the idea that one day I would own a pair of these speakers.

And like so many dreams, I put it aside while I got on with life. Until last year when the NAD amplifier finally gave up the ghost after twenty seven years of heavy use. A good life for an amplifier. After an extensive and intensive reading of the contemporary hi-fi literature (and I'd forgotten how much fun that can be), I plumped for a Yamaha AS 5000, a big black beast of an amp.

Of course the sensible solution with hi-fi is simply to replace the faulty part. A new amplifier to replace an old amplifier for instance. But one thing has a habit of leading to another with hi-fi. A new amplifier merely highlights any deficiencies in the input. So before I knew it, the amp was being driven by a new Yamaha CD 3000 CD player. Both sounded fantastic with lots of detail being teased out of the music. But of course this combo was calling out for something better than my existing speakers. "You know what you need" said a friend "electrostatic speakers".

Suddenly it was 1985 again and I was in the Charing Cross Road shop's basement listening to those electrostatic leviathans. A quick Google and I soon found out that the last ESL63 speaker left the Quad factory in 1999. In eighteen years Quad had made only thirty six thousand speakers. Eighteen thousand breeding pairs so to speak. That's three a day. Not exactly round-the-clock working. Each was essentially hand made. All of which suggested that the speakers would be rare. And therefore expensive. More googling seemed to support this - pairs sold privately for around one thousand five hundred pounds, a significant reduction on the original asking price but still way beyond my means. So near, yet so far. I switched off the computer.

"What about eBay?" Alice suggested.

And I have to say it had never crossed my mind. Ebay was surely for sewing machines, 1950s Barbie dolls, cigarette card collections and unwanted Lloyd Loom furniture. An online car boot sale. Not for top end precision electronics surely. A quick search revealed the breadth and depth of my misconceptions. Not only were there speakers for sale but also at very reasonable prices.

Catherine and Alice gave me a crash course in eBay bidding strategy. Watch rather than bid was the main part. So I watched auctions close without me bidding. Only when I had watched half a dozen sets of speakers go by was I allowed to bid. The girls singled out one particular pair of ESL63s for bidding.

"Why those?" I asked. They seemed the same as all the others.

"Easy. The speakers have been refurbished with new elements - they're basically new" said Alice, revealing a previously unnoticed affinity for the fine print.

"But they will go for a higher price then" I suggested.

"Nope" said Alice "look when the auction closes".

"But that's in the middle of the England-Scotland game" I said.

"Tada!" said Alice "everyone will be watching the rugby. Nobody will be bidding. Place an upper limit bid and forget about them"

So I did. Bid and forget. Until a week later, midway through an English lineout, my phone beeped. I was the winning bid and now owned a pair of essentially new ESL 63 electrostatics for an amazing five hundred and twenty one pounds.

"Told you" said Alice, still filing her nails. She looked up and smiled.

Three days later, a van pulled up outside and discharged two boxes, each the size of the monolith in "2001 -- A Space Odyssey". It took me less than half an hour to unpack and install the beasts. Well, I say install. What I actually mean is position these monsters in as unobtrusive a location as possible. In my haste to buy the things, it had somehow slipped my mind to tell Claire I had done so.

Two hours later, I met Claire at the door as she returned from work and explained that I had replaced the old speakers. And that the new ones were a tad bigger. In the living room, faced with speakers that shut out the light, she saw just what "a tad bigger" actually meant.

"Don't say anything" I said "sit down and listen".

I played the opening bars of Mahler's third Symphony. And Claire sat stock still as the brass fanfare rang out. Maybe a minute passed.

Then another.

"Oh my God" she said. "They're incredible".

Funnily enough, the same words I had used twenty seven years ago. I couldn't help but smile.

## 26 July 2012 - Speaking Dog

Dog owners take pride in the ability of their animal to respond to instructions. And indubitably, some dogs are very good. Some species too. Labradors are, and I realise I'm treading on thin ice here, widely reputed to be obtuse. Having said that of course, their use as guide dogs rather suggests otherwise. Poodles are often thought to be bright and I'm reliably assured by other members of the family that Louis, being a poodle, is in canine terms, an intellectual colossus. Moreover, being a bright poodle, he is, as near as makes no odds, a hyper intelligent pan dimensional being.

This notion, in the wake of overwhelming evidence to the contrary, grows ever more fanciful by the day. Look at the capacity to respond to instructions. For instance, take the command "sit", intended to establish a modicum of calm before a meal. Even the lowliest mutt can usually work this one out: Food or a similar treat is imminent and conditional upon placing of the backside on the ground. Simple. The same command however is interpreted by Louis as "sit still until the owner's back is turned, then shuffle briskly forwards on your bottom toward the food bowl". The same command, when getting overexcited in the garden (the dog, not me) is taken by Louis to mean "orbit the garden at high speed, deadheading the daffodils with your jaws, until you run into something hard, then yelp and whimper for several minutes". Hardly the behaviour of a hyper intelligent pan dimensional being. I've known lettuce that could respond better to orders.

"Stay" is another one. Again, this is not rocket science for the average canine. It means "don't budge until I tell you to". But not in Louis-speak. To Louis the command is interpreted as "sit down, stand up, sit down, stand up and repeat the cycle like a canine concertina until your owner loses the will to live".

"Come" is the command we use when calling Louis. Usually it signifies a reward for prompt adherence. But then again, how can you reward adherence, when Louis appears to hear "just wander around aimlessly beyond arm's reach in the largely vain hope that one or other of the children will chase after you".

Either way, this isn't working.

So I have decided to learn to speak dog. And based on the premise that language is the best learnt by imitation, I have been following Louis and repeating, verbatim mind you, his various barks, yelps, growls and snarls -- not that here are many of the latter.

This show of willingness is, perhaps inevitably, complicated by the fact that all barks sound the same. Many of the nuances of meaning, so obvious to another hyper-intelligent pan dimensional being are lost in the hands of humans. So I when I say to him "woof-woof-wooooooof", in the anticipation of it being something like "feel free to lick my nose", I am greeted by a couple of short barks, a brief howl and an unequivocal snarl.

Apparently, I said something about his sister.

## 31 July 2012 - Olympic Fever Take 2

I watched the opening ceremony on television. Or more accurately I watched part of it. And I'm none the wiser. I still haven't a clue what half of it was about. I quite liked the bit with the Queen jumping out of a helicopter and it was fun to see Mike Oldfield perform (I thought he was dead, honestly). But amid the huge set piece about Great Ormond Street, what kind of message does Voldemort and the child catcher send to our nation's sick children. " Sweet dream kids, try not to wet the bed" .

To be quite honest I was happy to watch proceedings on the telly. I hadn't actually intended to attend any particular event. But when the opportunity arose to go and watch some of the table tennis, we thought would give it a go. Alex and I are rather fond of table tennis. We have a table in the back garden and, although we tend not to play strictly according to the rules of table tennis, we do still enjoy it. So a chance to see how the world superstars play the game was an opportunity not to be missed.

Needless to say, the mere act of booking and collecting your tickets is probably a discipline worthy of consideration for the next Olympiad. Perhaps a new version of the decathlon.

Event 1: OLYMPIC TREASURE HUNT.
Find a sporting event or fixture that has not yet been sold out and does not make you look like Benny Hill for watching it (women's beach volleyball for instance).

Event 2: IDENTITY THEFT.
Find that you have to register with the website, before you can book anything. But only *after* you have spent nearly two hours making your detailed selections.

Event 3: NO FIXED ABODE.
Tap in your details to register only to find that the website refuses to accept your address, despite the fact they have been living there for the last 20 years.

Event 4: PARKY TIME TRIAL.
Finally tap in your detailed ticketing requirements, only to discover that the system has timed you out. The perils of having Parkinson's under time pressure.

Event 5: THE BIG SELL-OUT.
a bit of help, discover that half the events for which there are tickets available are now sold out in the time it took you to register your details.

Event 6: PRICE CHALLENGE.
Eventually manage to book 2 tickets for the table tennis round. Did you really mean to pay that much?

Event 7: CARD CARRIER.
Turn up at the venue to learn that you have to bring the credit card you used to book the tickets, and a photo ID in order to collect your tickets. Tough if they were a gift for friends

Event 8: THE MEDICATION SHUFFLE.
Negotiate airline style security while your medication goes off and the security guards begin to look interested in the shaky man.

Event 9: THE JAW DROPPER.
Discover that a bottle of Coca-Cola is a breathtaking two pounds thirty and a chicken wrap is six pounds.

Event 10: ENTENTE CORDIALE.
Take your seat among a large party of highly vocal group of supporters from one of those unknown republics somewhere in the Caucasus with the kind of flag that turns up in pub quizzes more often than the Olympics.

Despite the presence of the large party from Blogzhoffikazhaftklobberistan, who incidentally eat more garlic than can possibly be safe, we still managed to enjoy the proceedings. Although it did trigger Alex's hay fever again.

The rules appear to be very simple. The Chinese win. Unless you're Chinese, of Chinese descent, look a bit Chinese or have a Chinese-sounding name, you don't stand much of a chance. Go home now.

That certainly proved true for the British hopeful Paul Drinkhall who went out in straight sets to the German champion Maximilian Von Tirpitz (or whatever he was called). No need for penalties or whatever means they used to decide matches in this contest. I think his biggest problem was that he just simply played the game. To be a real champion in this sport you need to have clinical OCD. For instance, no self-respecting Oriental player would just throw the ball in the air and hit it. First the ball must be bounced exactly three times on the centreline, held in the palm of one's hand for exactly four seconds, rolled onto the table, picked up, bounced seven times on the floor and then served in a manner which reminded me of a chicken laying an egg.

The first time you see this, it is quite compelling. After the 20th time, you begin to see the point in the slow handclap emanating from certain sections of the audience. By the time the match has reached stalemate after three quarters of an hour, the entire crowd is rooting for his opponent. I don't suppose there has ever been a pitch invasion in table tennis that these kind of quirks will sometime provide the flashpoint. Mark my words.

Still, some of the matches were superb, the opponent barely separable in ability. Such was the case between the North Korean and South Korean players, a game played at the kind of intensity rarely seen off the battlefield. Indeed this was war by any other name. Alex was very impressed. "That North Korean looks as though he's playing for his life" he said.

The Russia-Croatia match was another that went down to the wire. Leonid Bolocsov eventually beat Vladimir Tosov after a match lasting about an hour and a half. Okay, I'll stop playing with the names. It was Andrej Gacina and he beat Alexander Shibaev in a pretty exciting match.

Of course the star of the day was Jike Zhang who dismissed some hapless Turk like an arctic fishermen clubbing a baby seal. It was pretty one-sided. But all these champions are used to playing on indoor tables set up with precision.

Our table at home presents something more substantial in the way of challenge. I wonder how Jike Zhang would fare then. If your shots are chosen to land with millimetre precision, how are you going to cope with the visible but uncorrected diagonal slope presented by our table? And don't think you can just call a timeout when a leaf lands on the table mid-point.

Or a gust of wind blows the ball off the edge.

Or, if you're unlucky enough to have the eastern end of the table (and what other end would you choose, Zhang) and find yourself squinting in the evening sun to see anything in the glare coming off the table.

It's also best not to make any sudden movements even if these are integral to your game. Louis interprets these as play and will try to trip you up. Or perhaps take a nip at your ankle. And let's see how you recover your composure after slipping on some previously unnoticed dog poo or tripping over one of Louis's bones.

Not so cocky now Zhang!

I'm just saying.

# AUGUST

**8 August 2012 – The civil war**

Parkinson's is not like heart disease or diabetes, although long-term chronic conditions themselves. Heart disease and diabetes may be challenges to the body. They may limit the things you can eat or do. But they leave no imprint on the psyche. They are, to all intents and purposes, invisible. You may have coronary artery disease or type II diabetes and still walk unnoticed in the street. You can be anonymous.

But Parkinson's is different. Whether you are a party animal or a hermit, Parkinson's marks you out as different. Children point. Adults look away from the blank faced shaky man. A tiny minority jeer or shout abuse, perhaps unsettled by the deviation from normality.

It's understandable. You are an embarrassment, freezing in doorways, unable to move and obstructing others. And unable to explain to the tut-tutting throng behind. Yes, Parkinson's is different.

Parkinson's is a civil war. Incidentally, as an aside, why is it called a 'civil' war when it is so very uncivil? But a civil war it is. Because Parkinson's is a war waged on your own brain, your own mind -- the very features that define you as a person.

And it is a guerrilla war, fought against an unseen enemy, flitting like shadows in the forests of the mind, picking off the neuronal stragglers.

War changes you. Parkinson's changes you and the very drugs you take to stay alive change you. In ways you would never guess. Sure they help you stride rather than shuffle and stand rather than sit. But their biggest effects are reserved for your mind. Some patients become obsessive, others withdrawn. Some have dreams, others nightmares. Some are lonely. Others are not short of company, with half-seen figures skirting the periphery of vision, playing Grandmother's footsteps with the edges of their minds.

It's no surprise. We take drugs with powerful actions on the limbic system, that ancient controller of our drives and urges. How can we be expected to stay the same amid these swirling neurochemical seas, like a boat tossed by waves. Of course we are different.

And there are times when you cry at the loss. At the high price you pay just to be able to walk.

But it's a tough gig for loved ones too. Because, whether they like it or not, this is their battle too. Drawn into another person's war on terms they did not choose, it should surprise nobody that marriage is often the first casualty.

And it's tough for friends. Fiends who have walked with you long enough to see the changes but are powerless to help. You hope your friends stick with you for as much of the journey as they can bear. Mine are well chosen and while I will never ask them to walk with me to the end of the pier, many would. So many support me – in little ways and more. Often they support me in ways even they do not realize. I am lucky.

Others are less fortunate. I know of one man with Parkinson's whose younger brother no longer spoke to him, perhaps spooked by his elder brother's frailty or stewing in some perceived grievance. Or affronted by what the medication had done to his sibling. He never knew. At a time when he needed his brother most, the brother answered no calls, replied to no letters or emails.

When Andrew died, taking his open-mouthed bewilderment to the grave, his widow, still bitter on her husband's behalf, never asked the brother to the funeral. As the rain fell on the grey late afternoon obsequies, Charles stood alone on the edge of the cemetery, until the mourners had filed away and the grave diggers came to finish their work.

Just another casualty in the war.

### 12 August 2012 – Stumps

As you know, I play cricket on Saturday for the 4th XI of my local club. For the last two years, I have also been the captain. I love it – I love the camaraderie, I love the banter and I love the strength of shared endeavor. Above all, I love playing cricket with Alex. I played cricket with my father and brother and I remember those days with huge affection. If my son has derived even a fraction of that same pleasure, it has been worthwhile.

But, that said, it has been a challenge even getting eleven players on the field on a Saturday. Despite the best efforts of the selection committee, players drop out with mystery viruses, exotic foreign holidays and visits to the vet. Usually on a Friday, leaving me facing a frenzied twelve hour telethon to find more suitable players. In the space of that time my definition of 'suitable' shifts from clones of Freddie Flintoff to anyone who knows which end to hold a bat. It matters naught that you have a glass eye, prosthetic leg and have never played cricket. After all, the captain has Parkinson's.

Inevitably the bits and pieces sides that take the field on a Saturday bear little resemblance to the formidable team picked by the selection committee on Tuesday. Sometimes we can be the 4th X or even the 4th IX.

On the field itself, this season has been exceptionally challenging. It's almost certainly a reflection of the advancement of the Parkinson's but the opposition bowlers seem younger, leaner and quicker, whizzing the ball past my bat noticeably more often and noticeably more rapidly than before. In the field, fewer catches seem within reach and those that are seem too fast to hold.

A few weeks ago, I reached a decision. If I'm honest, the decision reached itself - It was time to stop playing.

I wrote to the team:

*Over the last four seasons, I have had a wonderful time playing for this fantastic cricket club with as great a bunch of people as one could hope to meet.*

*Playing alongside my son and watching him develop as a cricketer has given me some of the happiest moments of my life. I saw him take his first senior wicket. I was there when he took his first senior hat trick. I watched with pride when he took seven for eight in a match. These are moments that are priceless and I thank the club.*

*Playing cricket with Parkinson's disease is, if I am honest, not easy. It is only thanks to a cocktail of nine medicines and supplements that I am able to walk, let alone play. However, the disease has now reached the stage where I am struggling to play cricket in any form.*

*With this in mind, I have notified the committee of my decision to resign as captain and retire as a player effective from 12th August.*

*I had hoped my health would hold long enough to collect my club cap for seventy five games but it's not to be. To be honest, I am happy to have played the fifty five I have. On 9th May 2009, when I played my first game, I would have settled for that.*

*Thanks guys, it's been a blast.*
*Jon*

I have been astonished by the warmth of the responses from other team and club members. Although written privately to me, the sentiments are so kind that I reproduce some of them anonymously here:

*I have really enjoyed playing cricket with you and your company over the last couple of years...*

*I really admire the courage and dignity that you have shown in fighting your terrible disease...*

*Thank you for your fantastic contribution to the club over the recent years...*

*You have been an inspiration, and held together the fourth eleven...*

*You've been an absolute inspiration to my entire family - of course C in particular, but the other children as well...*

*You have always been a good leader on the field. You taking catches in gully and slip in spite of your condition had always inspired me to do better...*

*It can't be easy to captain a 4th team at the best of times, but to take that job on while dealing with Parkinson's disease is a truly phenomenal effort...*

*Whilst the runs may have been fewer than you would have liked, you as a person and a captain have been an inspiration to your team and players, young and not so young...*

*We were very moved by your email and I'd like to take the opportunity of thanking you for welcoming us to the 4th XI and for giving us the opportunity to play cricket together...*

*I would like to say it has been a privilege to have played cricket over these last years with you..*

Believe me, the pleasure is entirely mine.

## 14 August 2012 - The Doncaster Dragons

Just off Station Road in Stainforth was an old prewar greyhound stadium, a rusting relic of a time when cloth-capped men like my great grandfather would keep and race whippets and greyhounds. Winning a shilling here, a tanner there -- and tearing down East Lane to the New Inn with enough to buy a round, except of course that this was Yorkshire and such munificence was unheard-of among the locals. Fat cat out-of-towners perhaps, flaunting florins and half crowns. In any case, you could spot the out-of-towners, with their sheepskin coats, Ford Zephyrs, and bottle blonde, caterpillar-lashed fancy women. They didn't impress us with their airs and graces.

Throughout its life, Doncaster Greyhound Stadium played host not only to greyhound racing but also to a host of low-budget automotive sports. There was banger racing, hot rods and stock cars. To many, the words hot rod might convey images of Corvettes, Mustangs and high-powered Dodges -- cars with supercharged eight litre engines, custom paint jobs, and vivid multicoloured sponsors' labels racing on the long roads through Nevada. But this was Stainforth, a pit village outside Doncaster, capable of dousing any such fantasy with a cold shower of Yorkshire reality, Here a hot rod was essentially a Ford Anglia or Mk I Cortina stripped of any chrome, and painted in whatever colour was on special offer that week in Armthorpe Paintmart. Turquoise emulsion most weeks. Or khaki.

A hacksaw resection of the silencer at least made the cars sound powerful. And to the eyes and ears of a ten-year-old Yorkshire schoolboy, the sight and sound of twenty such automotive ironclads jostling for position round a dog track was Doncaster's equivalent of the Monaco Grand Prix. Throw in a dodgy hot dog from Carlo's van (under which Beryl Goodall once found a dead rat) and the experience was indistinguishable from the Indianapolis 500. Well, if you were ten years old.

My father, one of the town's GPs, was often given tickets by grateful patients. And on a Saturday afternoon he would take me to see the town's young blades racing their cars round the greyhound stadium instead of up and down East Laith Gate at night. I particularly liked the bangers, cars even tattier than the hot rods. Banger racing had no rules. It was a case of last man standing. The cars would continue to bash into each other for hour upon wearying hour until only one could make it away from the affray under its own steam. "Something of a Pyrrhic victory" I once ventured to a bemused man stood next to me with a much annotated copy of The Racing Post. Not many of the punters drew parallels between banger racing and the military incompetence of pre-Christian kings of Macedonia.

But even this glittering array of automotive excitement paled by comparison with the spoils on offer in 1969. Because in 1969, for a fleeting two seasons, the greyhound stadium was host to a speedway team -- the improbably named Doncaster Dragons (briefly the Stallions) who paraded their motorcycling skills in the second division of the British speedway league (yes I was surprised to find that there was such a thing). And the Dragons could easily draw crowds upwards of two hundred thrill seekers if it was sunny. Maybe a quarter of that if it was raining. Fewer still if Carlo didn't bring the chip van.

Many of the riders were Polish, a connection that has never really seemed obvious to me. Certainly there was a big Polish community in Doncaster, mainly miners as you would expect. Perhaps mining was insufficiently dangerous and their thirst for needless peril could only be satisfied by hurtling round an oval circuit on a motorbike without any brakes. It looked incredibly dangerous. And it was. Hardly a meeting went by without one of the Dragons having their wings clipped. Fatalities were not uncommon.

Some riders donated their bodies to medicine, perhaps in thanks for their frequent recourse to the medical profession in life. My father's first dissection, in his second year at medical school was of a speedway rider who had come a cropper. In one class, the prescribed dissection was of the metacarpals, in particular their nerve supply. The anatomy instructor read out the details of the proposed procedure. Any questions? My father raised his arm and explained that such a dissection was not possible for him. Not that he was squeamish you understand – just that the cadaver was missing most of the right hand, torn off in the accident that claimed his life. And you could rule out anything below the knee for that matter.

In the post war period, many of the speedway riders were Polish ex-fighter pilots, used to danger at a different level. They never thought speedway dangerous – after all, it was the first time in five years they had not had someone firing machine guns at them.

Got a point.

## 22 August 2012 – The green hill

Saturday - off to Bayreuth for the Wagner with Rollo, JR and daughter Catherine. I am an excited kid. An early flight. Clearly Rollo and I are different. Before bedtime last night, I tell him we need to be on the road to Gatwick at 4am. Because of the hour, we will sneak out quietly. To me that would mean getting up at 3.45, quick wash and brushing of teeth and into the car, all further ablutions to be conducted en route. Not so Rollo. His alarm clock rings at 3am - an alarm that would have comfortably alerted shipping. Rollo fills the bathroom basin with water and the house with his own unique rendition of the major arias from Tannhauser. Never has the phrase 'special rendition' been more apt.

Inevitably, we arrive at the airport in plenty of time. Rollo is already fretting about breakfast and the availability of food at the departure gates. Normally I'm the one, Mr Shakyshuffles, who attracts the interest of the airport security but not today. Today, for whatever reason, it is Rollo who is to be frisked, swabbed and X-rayed. He emerges from their clutches having narrowly avoided the Marigolds. The security guards are also surprised to be asked about breakfast. We settle for a bacon roll and an espresso each. Rollo perks up.

Two hours later we are in Munich. When JR's flight from Malta arrives an hour or so later, Rollo is already beginning to make noises about lunch so the three of us settle for bratwurst and sauerkraut at the sports bar. Even after six bratwurst apiece, it seems churlish to resist strudel. Rollo is eying up the Sachertorte.

We pick up the car keys from Europcar and directions to its location in the car park. The teutonic veneer of calm and efficiency is cracked a moment later when a flustered Europcar assistant appears. 'You vait please. Ze car ees on fire'. Ve vait.

Still we wait. Four fire engines and an ambulance appear. They seal off the car park in a blitzkrieg operation and set about dowsing all the top-of-the-range Mercedes they can find. No reason - they just enjoy their job. After half an hour of this cabaret, the car park is reopened. We find the car and it becomes obvious that the rental assistant had confused the definite and indefinite articles in her message. Our car is not even smouldering.

Two hours later, the familiar shape of the Festspielhaus, standing proud on the grunen hugel looms into view. We are in Bayreuth, having safely negotiated the A9 which, on the evidence of some of the driving we saw, is clearly an extension of the Nurburgring.

It is thirty one degrees, eighty eight in old money. Not a cloud in the sky. The hotel does not have air conditioning. In former times, Rollo, JR and I would have automatically headed for the first bar and drunk dunkelbier until our heads hurt. When you are young, this seems almost mandatory. But with a cumulative age pushing a hundred and sixty, we are a little more circumspect. A siesta, a shower and a shave takes an hour or two and, when we meet in the lobby, our thoughts are leaning more toward an early supper and early night rather than life-endangering volumes of Bavarian pilsner. Life's clock runs slower.

We settle on Oskar's halfway down Maximilianstrasse for a 'light snack'. This phrase, of course, has no meaning in Bavaria and we are soon faced with mountains of food. My pork hock is the size of a rugby ball while Rollo's schnitzel is nearly A4. Both go down well with a couple of 'dunkels'.

Nonetheless, it is clear that a diet consisting solely of pig pieces, dumplings and beer will be a belt-busting course of action, even if only for three days. I point this out at breakfast. More dietary balance is needed. Rollo nods, pours himself a small glass of orangensaft and returns to the table with a 'there, that will do it' sort of look. He has a sixty page synopsis of Lohengrin in front of him and is in no mood to let a coronary get between him and his Wagner.

### 25 August 2012 – Destination Valhalla

It's Sunday and tonight's treat at the Festspielhaus is Lohengrin, a four hour mediaeval swords-and-sorcery bash featuring, in the blue corner, Miss Goody Two Shoes, Elsa von Brabant. Pitched against her, in the red corner, and demonstrating conclusively that Wagner's baddies are always his most interesting characters, is the scheming witch Ortrud. It's a heavyweight bout. Two Wagnerian sopranos on one stage! Something has to give.

The plot consists mainly of swans, magic, sword fights, and lots of animated accusations. Into the middle of all this hocus pocus comes Lohengrin, a knight of the Holy Grail, who marries Elsa on the condition that she never asks his true name. My first reaction is that this will make signing the register difficult at the very least but nobody, least of all Wagner, seems to have thought of this. Still,

Lohengrin won't be the first husband in history to learn to respond to "Oy, you". In any case it's an excuse for a knees-up.

Inevitably, within an hour of exchanging vows, Elsa blots her copy book and asks his name "It's Wayne, isn't it? Or Darren". Lohengrin soon tires of playing Twenty Questions and calls a press conference to announce his name to anyone who cares. Ortrud and the baddies, who have money on "Elvis" at eighty five to one, turn up too. Predictably it all kicks off and, by the end, the key players in the drama are, for the most part, dead. Lohengrin, without a hint of social responsibility, waltzes off in a swan boat, leaving much blubbing among the girlies and an astronomical bar bill. Great music but, with the best will in the world, a pretty wonky plot.

This already flaky plot is rendered even more bizarre by a staging in which most of the characters are wearing laboratory rat costumes. No, really. There is, needless to say, no precedent for this in the opera. Nevertheless, as neither Rollo, JR nor I have seen Lohengrin before, we are looking forward to it hugely. Rats or no rats. But before we get there, we have to fetch Catherine, the last of our party. Claire has generously surrendered her Bayreuth ticket to our musician daughter who, in any case, has been studying Wagner at college.

The logistics are complex - Catherine has been playing a concerto on the Saturday and therefore could not travel with Rollo and I. She has been spared Rollo's early morning Tannhauser medley and is on the redeye from Gatwick to Munich on Sunday. To cut a long story short, JR and I drive to Nuremburg to collect her at lunchtime on Sunday.

Clear roads mean we are early. We stop for half an hour at the infamous Zeppelin field. Even decayed, the stadium has an uncomfortable presence. The terraces have gradually become banks of wild flowers while the concrete of the dais and colonnades slowly crumble, permitted only such maintenance as to make the structures safe. Although now mainly used by enthusiastic youths with skateboards and roller blades, and visited by a handful of tourists, there was a time when this place echoed to different voices with darker passions and beliefs.

Catherine is waiting for us in designer sunglasses, bassoon on her back, and cooling herself with a strawberry fan. The temperature is now an egg frying thirty nine degrees Celsius or a hundred and two degrees fahrenheit.

By the time we reach the Festspielhaus, in our glad rags and ready for action, this has fallen to a mere ninety nine degrees Fahrenheit. A temperature barely worth a mention except for the fact that we are all in dinner jackets, our seats are in the balcony and the Festspielhaus has no air conditioning. We may look like penguins but we do not feel like them. This is going to be tough.

By the end of the first act, I know just how tough it is going to be. My meds have the side effect of lowering my blood pressure and making the blood pool in my ankles. A minor irritation most of the time but a bigger problem if you throw in vasodilation, low blood sugar levels and a little dehydration. Add an inability to move - due to the opera not the Parkinson's - and things can turn nasty.

After an hour, I know I am in trouble. My shirt is drenched, sweat is pouring into my eyes, and I can feel the tell tale signs of fainting as my peripheral vision closes in and my ears ring. Somehow I make it to the end of the Act. Rollo and JR are concerned enough to fetch lemon sorbet. But I clearly won't make it to the end of the opera. There is also the small matter of the tickets. At £150, you do not surrender the things lightly. I phone Catherine, who was sitting out Lohengrin, to put on her frock and some lippy and hotfoot it to the Festspielhaus. The third act is hers. I will find a cool shady place nearby and rehydrate.

This proves prudent. Bayreuth frequently claims victims. It's understandable - the audience is pretty old and the temperature in the theatre is oppressive. So sitting out the third act is common sense not common cowardice. Catherine gets her first experience of Wagner and I live to fight another day. Which is more than can be said for the poor fellow I see stretchered out shortly after the bridal chorus. A blue flash dash.

Go direct to Valhalla. Do not pass Go.

## 27 August 2012 – Toro Rosso

Last night's ill health during Lohengrin has left me with some serious thinking to do. I am anxious to avoid a repeat performance. Good friends that they are, Rollo and JR are also determined to avoid any further problems for me during tonight's offering on the green hill. Especially since it will be just as warm today. Rollo, who is sitting out tonight, will be our support team. His allotted task is to make sure we - Catherine, JR and myself - keep ourselves in as good a shape as possible during tonight's opera.

Never has this support been more essential than during tonight's performance. Because the opera in question is Tristan und Isolde, one of Wagner's longest meisterwerks and one of my particular favourites.

To cut a long story short, the opera opens with Tristan ferrying Isolde to Cornwall to marry his boss King Mark, having already killed Isolde's boyfriend before the curtain has even risen. Needless to say, Tristan is not on Isolde's Christmas card list. And she doesn't fancy being Queen of Cornwall. She is, it has to be said, pretty high maintenance in mediaeval terms.

Still cross over that little boyfriend-killing episode, she decides to murder Tristan and herself with a poison drink, der Totentrank. All well and good. But her maid, the well-intentioned but rather soft in the head Brangaene, substitutes a love potion, der Liebestrank. Tristan and Isolde fall madly in love with each other, a state of affairs that is at best highly inconvenient, bearing in mind their domestic and employment circumstances. Oops says Brangaene. My bad.

From here, things pretty much run the expected course. Four hours of opera later, Tristan and Isolde are dead - which they would have been anyway if Brangaene had not swapped the potions. The opera would have been three hours shorter though.

Would Tristan and Isolde have fallen in love without being drugged by the love potion? Who knows. Who cares. Whether due to love or other drugs, the result is an excuse for some of the most sumptuous music Wagner ever wrote, especially so in the second act, an introspective bubble of self-absorbed passion containing, in my humble opinion, the most beautiful love duet in musical history.

I'm babbling. I like Wagner. You know that.

But my immediate problem is less the psychological tensions of the plot than the need to get through nearly five hours of Wagner in a sweltering opera house without (a) falling asleep, (b) passing out or (c) desperately needing the toilet. In the light of the Lohengrin, experience, you could probably add "(d) dying" to the list of possible negative outcomes.

We need something that will sustain blood sugar levels and be reasonably invigorating. After much deliberation, we conclude that this will best be achieved by a combination of Red Bull and Jaffa cakes, taken before the opera and repeated during each interval. Rollo is on hand to administer to us.

By the end of the opera, I have consumed three cans of Red Bull and eleven Jaffa cakes. This prescription proves astonishingly effective. My innate propensity for operatic somnolence is completely suppressed. I sail through the opera without problems. I am not only awake throughout each act, but alert and attentive. The strategy is a triumph. I feel great.

The following day however, the strategy looks a mite less brilliant. We are leaving Bayreuth for France and, by the time we arrive at the airport, I have been awake for thirty four hours and counting. All well and good if I had been going to an all-night rave but, by any standard of uninterrupted wakefulness a high price to pay for yesterday's triumph. Frankly, I look like death.

So much for Red Bull. I'll make it a Totentrank next time.

### 31 August 2012 - Barry boys

I like classic cars. Always have. Sports cars snarling like wild animals. Big lazy luxury saloons, like gentleman's clubs on wheels. Italian cars, elegant but unreliable, all style without substance. 1950s American chrome leviathans. Saloon cars, sports cars, shooting brakes, racing cars, limousines. Anything built with quality and loved by its owner.

Of course few get to own a classic Lamborghini or Cadillac Eldorado. For the most part, we have to settle for more run of the mill transportation, perhaps personalising our cars with some elegant little flourish, some small touch. Perhaps a leaper for a Jaguar for instance. Or a sport steering wheel for a classic MGB.

But there are some for whom this ... er... personalisation knows no bounds. People so determined to make their car stand out from the pack that they will stop at nothing. These young men - and it is always men between seventeen and twenty five - lose all insight into their vehicles as they lash on a spoiler, paint the car orange or add go faster stripes. It is the automotive equivalent of tattoos and piercings. The possibilities are as limitless as the results are comical. No modification is too extreme.

The desired objective - to make a small undernourished, bottom of the range hatchback look like an American muscle car - is, of course never going to succeed. No chance. A 1.1L Vauxhall Corsa will never pass for a Dodge Viper, no matter what you do to it. Apart from sell it. And a Volkswagen Polo with cheap alloys, racing number and tea tray spoiler will always look more like Herbie than a

Porsche Carrera. These efforts are universally doomed to failure.

But where I despair of these automotive tragedies, Alex and his friend Tom have become connoisseurs of the genre (Barry Boys, they call them), constantly photographing and charting these crimes against automotive humanity. So extensive has their study been, and so profound their scholarship, that they have even developed a points system, the bones of which I feel compelled to share with you.

Points are awarded for all non-showroom modifications on the basis of three key criteria - (a) lack of necessity, (b) absence of resulting function and (c) incompetence of execution. The more jarringly inappropriate or outright dangerous the modification, the higher the mark. For instance a simple spoiler earns a miserly five points. A large spoiler gets you ten. A giant spoiler the size of a picnic table with vertical fins is at least a twenty point payout. If the spoiler appears to have been attached by either superglue, bluetack or double-sided sellotape, further bonus points are on offer. The sky's the limit.

First things first. Let's start with the basics. The car. Obviously it needs to be small and underpowered. This will help make subsequent modifications all the more futile. Look for Corsas, Puntos, Novas, Micras, Polos and bottom end Golfs. If you can find an old XR2 so much the better but these are Barry Boy gold dust these days.

This is just the starting point. To qualify as a Barry Boy, Alex and Tom have determined that you need at least three of the folllowing: Matt black bonnet, go faster stripes, spoiler, LED lights, cheap alloys, roll cage, darkened glass, sport steering wheel, replacement light clusters and fat tyres. And while you are at it, please remove the manufacturer and model badges. If necessary, replace with "V8", "Sport" or just "R", but only as long as the car is not a V8.

Colour is important too. Do not dally with anything from the showroom colour palette. Bright crayon primary colours (or purply pearlescent) are de rigeur. Banana yellow and vivid orange are good solid choices but, for the full 30 points, it has to be lime green. If you can't make other road users sick with envy, just sick will do.

Exhausts are Barry essentials. Twin exhausts are an easy ten points, quadruples are twenty (but only if unconnected to the engine). Wide bore exhausts like jet outlets are also twenty. Air intakes are also a rich source of points, but only if cosmetic. An intake on the bonnet will earn you fifteen points while air inlets cut into the bodywork ahead of the rear wheel arches to suggest rear-engined grunt are an automatic twenty points each. Additional marks can be earned if the appended bodywork looks particularly amateurish. Lack of taste can only take you just so far. Sometimes you need that edge that only true incompetence can provide.

The same goes for skirting. For full marks, this should reach to within an inch of the ground, like a solid wall of fibreglass. If it is a different colour to the bodywork, even better. If it is clearly designed for a different car, the points on offer are almost limitless, determined only by the extent of the mismatch. And if you are contemplating skirts, don't rule out lowering the suspension. With a little attention to detail, it should be impossible to tell if the scraping sound is coming from the skirting or the wheel arches. Both are equally dangerous and therefore worthy of full marks. If skirting is too difficult, consider blue under-car lighting. Almost impossible to do tastefully and thus twenty easy points. Most attempts at blue LED lighting look like the frozen fish counter at Iceland.

On the subject of noise, one should not underestimate the points value of a truly insane sound system, with speakers the size of refrigerators sequestered in the boot. Ideally this should be playing gangster rap or, at the very least, music that suggests you are capable of greater misdemeanours than dropping sweet wrappers in the street. You won't hear too many Val Doonican records from a Barry Boy.

The essence of Barry Boy motoring can be encapsulated in the epithet "If you can't take a joke, don't drive one". Remember, the idea is to spend a king's ransom on modifications that will make the car look pants.

Oh and one last thing - don't forget the fluffy dice. Thirty points.

# SEPTEMBER

**3 September 2012 - Fifty shades of magnolia**

For the last several weeks all I have heard about is Fifty Shades of Grey. Yes, that book. Worldwide multisquillion seller and, as far as I can tell, every woman on earth's holiday reading. The airport bookshops can't shift them fast enough, so much does demand outstrip supply. Apparently it outsells Harry Potter, proving that there is more than one kind of magic wand, I guess.

And no female seems immune. Normally rational women are going weak at the knees over the book, forming ad hoc reading groups to dawdle over its content with a glass of Pinot Grigio. High-powered captains of industry are becoming screaming schoolgirls again, gripped by a sort of collective literary Beatlemania.

It is, I'm repeatedly assured, a brilliant modern love story, with finely drawn characters. A passionate depiction of modern relations. A masterpiece of early 21st century fiction even.

Really?

Am I missing something here? Is this truly a literary masterpiece? Will it, a century from now, stand alongside Anna Karenina as one of literature'a great love stories? Will it be part of the English Literature GCSE syllabus? Will we speak of its author in the same breath as Chaucer, Shakespeare and Dickens?

Or is it just a smutty Mills and Boon? A writing-by-numbers exercise with a bit more willy waving. Barbara Cartland with a bit of S & M, if that isn't too disturbing an image?

Global sales of megabucks and a readership of millions for this? Do you think I'm jealous?

You bet I am.

### 5 September 2012 - Overlord

Scattered among the breakers at Arromanches les Bains are the remnants of the pontoon bridges and 'Phoenixes', huge concrete blocks that formed the Mulberry harbour and allowed supplies ashore to support the D-Day invasion beach heads. And stretching east, toward Courseulles, lies Gold Beach where, in the early hours of

June 6 1944, some twenty five thousand British soldiers of the 50th Infantry Division came ashore as part of Operation Overlord.

Catherine, called back to Blighty early from our family holiday in Brittany by college commitments, was booked on the eleven o'clock evening sailing from Caen and we had decided to make an afternoon of it. A pleasant drive, a bit of history, and a good meal.

We parked in a side street in Arromanches and ambled down to the Musee de la Debarquement. And although we were jostled by a rather strident tour group keen to get their money's worth, we still found plenty to interest. Bombs, mines, models, uniforms and maps aplenty. Natural territory for the boys but surprisingly engaging for the girls too it seems, perhaps dwelling more on the human side of the drama than the hardware on display. Hard to believe that this was nearly seventy years ago.

We dined at a small bistro at the far west end of the Rue Joffre behind the beachfront. Although suspicious of eateries on the tourist track, I was very pleasantly surprised. Their set menus, named after pertinent local aspects of the landings, were excellent. I chose Le Menu Overlord and, since I was driving and the new French drink-drive laws are punitive, washed it down with a citron presse. I plumped for whelks, which sound infinitely more seductive as bugots a l'aioli, followed by a travers de porc au miel (slow-roasted pork ribs glazed in honey) and a teurgoule de Normandie (a rich local rice pudding). Universally delicious.

The Normandy coast, from Barfleur to Deauville, is littered with the debris of D-day and the weeks that followed. On the beaches, long clear of mines, children play among the poignant remnants of the landings. We followed the D514 coast road to Ouistreham, passing Juno and Sword beaches, dropping Catherine at the ferry port a little after nine, among a rowdy bunch of French exchange students, excited to be going to l'Angleterre. Catherine plugged herself into the Wifi and settled down to what I imagine was as little sleep, but for different reasons, as on that moonless June night in 1944.

The First World War has already passed into history. No survivors of that conflict remain to speak of the horrors of Ypres, The Somme and Paschendaele. But the Second World War is still in living memory. Old soldiers still relive their fears, talk of the hailstorm of bullets they faced on those beaches, and tell of those whose stories ended there on the sand. And throughout Normandy, in the hinterland behind the coastline, are dotted cemeteries containing the remains of over one hundred and thirty thousand young men for whom The Battle of Normandy was their last campaign. Most, some eighty thousand, are German.

As Albert Schweitzer famously said "War cemeteries are the greatest communicators of peace".

### 8 September - Team JS

Parkinson's may not be my choice exactly but I do at least have some idea of how to deal with the little blighter. OK it still manages to spring the odd surprise and I have the feeling its bag of tricks is far from exhausted. But, in a manner of speaking at least, it's still my gig. It's part of me and, whether or not I read the small print on this particular contract, it's here to stay. Like some unwanted timeshare in Benidorm, I'm stuck with it.

But there are others who did not sign up for Parkinson's. My wife and children did not. At no point was Claire asked whether she wanted a husband with an incurable neurological illness. Nobody checked to see if Catherine needed a father who walked like a drunk, mumbling and stumbling. Or if Alice was happy with a dad who fell asleep at dinner and quivered like a poplar in a breeze. Did Alex feel comfortable having the only dad who couldn't play football?

Let's face it – that's NO across the board. All the kids really wanted (and, until 2006, largely got) was a normal dad, one who didn't draw attention to himself with seismic shakes or flailing arms. And who can blame them - when you are a teenager, these things matter. Who wants Windmill Dad.

Sure, we take medication to reduce the shakes or loosen our robotic limbs. But the price of calm is high because Parkinson's, and its treatments lest we forget, changes those who have it. Families and friends are as frustrated by the mood swings and impulsivity as we are, dismayed by the self-absorption, symptoms we may hardly notice. It takes fresh eyes to see what we don't, fresh mouths to tell us what we need to know and fresh ears to listen where we do not hear.

In so many ways our families and loved ones 'suffer' from Parkinson's more than those diagnosed with the condition. They witness, but can little change the slow retreat.

They may be shocked witnesses to the damage this condition causes or they may be front line soldiers in the fight, supporting and helping in what ways they can. There will be times when they may be both. And at other times neither. Whether they would have made these choices is of course wholly irrelevant because, like it or not, they have been drawn into a conflict that was not of their choosing. Welcome to team JS.

## 11 September 2012 - Legless

Like much of the country, I have been engrossed in the Paralympics on television. So when Anton asked me if I wanted to watch the athletics at the Olympic Stadium itself, I jumped (metaphorically) at the chance. So there we were - Anton and his son Tom, Alex and myself - spending Wednesday evening watching the track and field. We saw wheelchair races, the bladerunners, wheelchair- bound shotputters and, best of all, the blind javelin throwers. Some of those guys throw over sixty metres. Inevitably, bearing in mind that they are throwing blind, there is quite a scatter. The field judges were certainly very attentive. And when the announcer called for silence to help the blind athletes, you could have heard a pin drop. Apart from a couple of idiots who had clearly spent too long in the beer tent and were heckling some of the amputees. The police soon discouraged them. Ironic that the only people who caused any trouble were, in their own way, legless.

And I have to say of the athletes that these chaps (and chapesses) are amazing. Amazing in the many ways they have overcome adversity. Amazing in the way they have adapted to change. And amazing in the positive outlook and spirit they consistently exhibit.

Just how do you swim without arms? How do you play football when blind? How do you play rugby in a wheelchair? In each case, the answer is the same - with an indomitable will and fierce determination. And many have had to cope with sudden disability, often encountered in traumatic circumstances. A roadside bomb in Afghanistan for instance. Make no mistake, these are extraordinary people.

So I ask which came first? Were these men and women already strong, willful and driven, shrugging their injuries aside as they focused on a new field of endeavour? Or were they more aimless, only waiting for the right stimulus to fire their imagination? Do you need both? There are no half empty glasses here.

But what strikes me most is just how unfailingly cheerful these athletes are. Who can forget Hannah Cockcroft's beaming smile and excited post-race babble? Or Jonnie Peacock's rather too easily lipread expression of victory? Or the bladerunner Oscar Pistorius wrapped in the South African flag after winning the four hundred metres? Magical. Even those who did not win - and who would dare call them losers - were positive, simply thrilled to be a part of it all.

There is a message here in the courage, optimism and enthusiasm of these athletes - that determination will carry the day. If you want something enough, you will not be thwarted by obstacles in your way. If life gives you lemons, make lemonade.

Parkinson's is not so different. It disables too. And I hear the message of the paralympians. Loud and clear. So what if life in a wheelchair beckons, it's not the end. It's a beginning of something else. Adapt. I will not, I repeat not, fail to learn that lesson.

And I pledge here and now that I will fight on to find a cure for Parkinson's. Today and tomorrow. Next month and next year.

No surrender.

## 14 September 2012 - The fledgling

Alice is ready for college life. In fairness she has been ready for ages, with a summer mostly spent prowling around the house like a caged beast during the daylight hours and partying and clubbing long and hard into the night while waiting for her A-level results.

In the end, despite many sleepless nights for her and her parents (albeit for different reasons), Alice got the A-level grades she needed and secured a place at her first choice of university. She was delighted. We were delighted. Alex, whose relationship with Alice is often stormy, was delighted. Only Catherine, secretly hoping Alice would get her second choice and therefore be in London with her, was slightly subdued. But, all things considered, a very good outcome. Alice is off to university.

And so it comes round again. Echoes of Catherine's leaving in 2010 and the realisation that we, her parents, are the only people in the universe who still see our little Alice as a child in need of our help and guidance. She is not and, more to the point, has not been for some time. She is eighteen, a grown woman, and able to tell us when (or, more accurately, if) she needs our advice. We would do well to button it. We cannot guide, advise, suggest, propose, question, comment, order, decide or control. Those staples of modern parenting, bold pillars of Parental Wisdom, are no longer applicable.

In the words of Shakespeare…

*All the world's a stage.*
*And all the men and women merely players:*
*They have their exits and their entrances;*
*And one man in his time plays many parts.*

And with it comes the understanding that we are now mere spectators in the great play of Alice's life. New players will strut on Alice's stage, new actors in the drama of her life. New characters will play their parts as the drama unfolds. Bit parts, cameos and leads.

Because this play is not about us. Alice is the leading lady.

But we will always be there, waiting in the wings, unseen. Following the play and trying to read ahead, to foresee the unforeseeable. Ready to applaud her successes and to catch her when she falls. And knowing that we will not be the first to hug her with joy. Nor the first handkerchief to dab away a tear. Those roles will fall to others.

Birds teach their offspring to fly by example. There is no practice for life. Nestlings flap their wings in imitation until the day comes when they stand, as fledglings, on the edge of the nest. Their parents watch in nervous anticipation, chirping encouragement. And in that moment, between nest and flight, is crystallised everything they have ever been as parents. Every lesson they hope has been taught. Every crumb of useful wisdom. Everything that will equip the young fledgling for life.

Time to fly.

## 17 September – A Scottish wedding

The Lowlands. Centuries of skirmishing have moved the border so often in this part of the Northeast that nobody can say with certainty what is Scotland and what is England any more. Nonetheless, a sign outside Coldstream confidently welcomes the visitor to Scotland and, for the most part, this location will serve as well as any.

Speaking of centuries of skirmishing, this was, in a manner of speaking, the purpose of the trip to Kelso, to attend the wedding of Callum, an old friend of some two decades, to the beautiful and feisty Victoria.

The stag do, sensibly held some weeks earlier, had been, by all accounts, a well lubricated golf-fest. Golf is, I'm reliably assured, a thirsty game. According to one unnamed source, the rounds of golf increased in direct proportion to the rounds at the bar – Eagles and birdies became bogies and albatrosses. The discovery of Jagerbombs probably didn't help. On the final morning, the club secretary, his patience tested beyond human endurance, reached for his tannoy to berate one of the miscreant party:

"Will the gentleman on the women's tees, please move back 20 yards to the men's tees".

The gentleman concerned turned round, put his club down and shouted back

"Will the gentleman with the megaphone please be quiet while I take my second shot"

Mercifully, I was not part of the stag bash -- this was restricted to a select band of hard-drinking golfopaths. In any case, having met Dougal and Ronald at the wedding, two of the ringleaders, it is clear that any attempt to match them drink for drink would entail loss of life. Mine.

Kelso, our destination, is not well-served by public transport. So we took the train to Berwick on Tweed, a journey made more tiring by a group of Spanish students who crowded the aisles, babbling excitedly in a mix of English and Catalan for nigh on four hours. Bizarrely, Berwick, not known for bellicosity, has an entry in the Guinness Book of Records, for the longest recorded period of sustained hostilities. One hundred and thirteen years. Due to a diplomatic oversight, Berwick somehow omitted to sign the Crimean War armistice in 1856, a situation unresolved formally until 1966. Not a lot of people know that.

Callum's elder brother Jacob collected us from the station and kindly drove us to Kelso. This is a picturesque part of the world at any time of year, but particularly so on this late autumnal afternoon as, screwing up our eyes against the low sun, we passed fields of fire, burnished gold hedgerows, and coppered copses.

The hotel, set back from the cobbled street, was a rather grand, former baronial hall built in 1741, the wood panelled walls bedecked with hunting and fishing trophies. Backing onto the Tweed, the hotel was a microcosm of Monarch-of-the-Glen Scotland, even boasting its own smokery, beehives and distillery. A wood fire burned in the bar and the kedgeree for breakfast was the best I've ever eaten. Having said that, the plumbing for the hotel, most of which appeared to be routed though the wall space behind my bedhead, sustained a growling rumble throughout the hours of darkness at the kind of decibel level associated with cruise missile launches.

Still It is great that these quirky family-owned hotels continue to exist, fighting for individuality against a tide of commercial blandness. I shudder to think what Marriott, Hilton or Novotel would do to the place if it ever fell into their clutches.

Callum and Victoria were married the following afternoon in Polwarth Kirk, a tiny austere country church, on a windswept hillside in the middle of nowhere. In fact, so remote is the church that it has been closed for several years and may only be used on special occasions with the permission of the estate owner. As we approached the church, set in a small tumbledown graveyard, the strains of a lone piper drifted our way, caught on the breeze. And in this place were Callum's roots. His grandmother had been married here too a century ago. Parts of the church date back to 1242 records suggest a church on the site as far back as 900 A.D.

The minister's wife chatted to us while her husband, a late vocation formerly a city stockbroker, shepherded us into the kirk, out of the strengthening breeze. She was pleased to have had picked a plain, narrow brimmed red hat rather than the huge construction covered with feathers and furs her husband had proposed . "It looked like roadkill" she said, rolling her eyes heavenward.

On the whole, the wedding was a largely hat free zone, perhaps a nod to the generally windy conditions. Being Scottish, inevitably the kilts outnumbered the hats by about 3 to one. And although more than one of the women guests found themselves wearing the same frock, no such fashion faux pas applied to the kilts. Each was subtly different and, to a mere Sassenach, surprisingly subdued in colours -- more Braveheart than Brigadoon. I asked Callum if he was wearing the family tartan. He had intended to, but it turned out that neither he nor twin brother John had been able to get into their own kilts and had been forced to hire. I should add here that both brothers are giants of men, built like grizzly bears. Nonetheless, the sight of twin brothers wearing different tartans was rather dislocating. At least one of them has to be wrong. But which?

I'm sure Scots must never tire of being subjected to questions on the wearing or not of sub-kilt underwear. Even here, more than one English lady was heard to ask "What's worn beneath a kilt?" The best reply I overheard was "Nothing's worn – it's all in perfect working order".

But while the kilts were rather muted, the same could not be said for the sporrans. While some were little more than chic designer purses, other more traditional examples appeared to be fashioned from large sections of animal hide, adorned with fur and tassles. The simpler forms might barely have held enough change for a parking meter, whilst the more flamboyant examples would probably have accommodated the parking meter itself.

The wedding breakfast – why do they call it that, at 5pm? – was delicious and the speeches were excellent (as well as being a rich source of material for this). Callum even kindly acknowledged me in his speech as his research mentor. And when it came to the ceilidh that ended the evening, the kilts proved to be in a league of their own. Evidently Scottish country dancing is an inherited genetic skill. You can either do it or you can't. Don't try to fake it. Young and old alike joined in. And the band called all sorts of airs, jigs and reels. Even Ronald was enticed onto the dance floor, although by this stage in the evening and rather the worse for wear, every dance involving Ronald appeared to be a reel.

Around one o'clock in the morning, proceedings wound up with the entire wedding party joining hands to sing Auld Lang Syne. A heartwarming end to a joyful day.

Then all was quiet.

Apart from the cruise missile launches in Room 48.

**19 September 2012 - If we shadows have offended**

I had asked a painter from the local council to paint the exterior woodwork of our house, which had begun to deteriorate. Being September already and busy enough that he could only spare a single day, he turned up with two assistants. They set about the window frames, barge boards and guttering with some gusto but little technique. To be honest, they were a little hasty and shoddy in their work with many drips on the paving outside.

In order that they did not miss any details on the window closures, the foreman asked me to open all the upstairs windows. I had a concert that evening and, as the afternoon wore on, I began to fret that they would not finish the work in time for me to close the windows and make the house secure before leaving.

I changed into my dinner jacket and went to the bathroom to check my appearance and brush my hair. All good.

As I emerged from the bathroom, I saw some movement in my bedroom. One of the men was inside the room painting the bedroom door frame. He must have climbed through the window. I turned round and another man was in Alice's room.

I assumed there had been a misunderstanding and that the painters were also contracted to paint the inside of the house too. It was all rather confusing.

The first man had made a mess. There was no tarpaulin and I could see paint drops on the carpet. I was livid and shouted to him to stop.

"You are dripping on the carpet" I said "look at the mess".

He paused, dipped his brush in the paint and advanced toward me.

"Call that a mess?" he laughed and shook his head. "This is a mess, mate".

Before I could open my mouth to speak he pushed the brush in my face and drew it down over my dinner jacket.

"You'll be a fine sight at the prom, won't you" he said, his face so close I could smell the alcohol.

I don't know if I was more frightened or angry but I do remember missing with my first punch. My second caught him on the cheekbone, just below the eye and the third and fourth landed with a disabling crunch on his nose and jaw.

There were loud shrieks and a shout of "Jon - stop!" in a woman's voice. It was Claire.

It was dark and I was lying down. I stopped fighting and lay still, catching my breath. It took me a second or two to realise where I was in the half light of dawn.

For most people, dreams may be vivid but do not become real. During REM sleep, the period in which we dream, the body is still. Inhibitory descending pathways block muscle movement to prevent dreams being enacted. This is thought to be an evolved protection mechanism.

Acting out dreams is not uncommon in Parkinson's. Changes in the input and output circuitry of the basal ganglia are so profound in Parkinson's that this should come as no surprise. The drugs that we take and the condition itself contribute to these thespian outbursts. And it is our bedfellows that bear the brunt of this.

In the words of Puck, from Shakespeare's A Midsummer Night's Dream...

*"If we shadows have offended,*
*think but this and all is mended,*
*that you have but slumbered here*
*while these visions did appear"*

I know of one woman who woke to find her (Parkinsonian) husband trying to strangle her. He was a big man and she might so easily not have woken. Even though he too was acting out a dream, it was a terrifying moment and pretty much spelt the end of their marriage.

I apologised to Claire. What else could I do. Fortunately I am no Muhammad Ali and the pillow had taken the brunt of the attack.

"I'm really sorry" I said "that was bad".

"It's worse than that" said Claire "your left hook is rubbish".

## 22 September 2012 - Thirty three

I've always liked food. And I think I can trace my current girth to the kind of nutritional liberation I experienced at university.

Firstly, for the first time in my life, what I ate was my choice. School dinners were a thing of the past. And good riddance. Breakfast apart, the grim grey catering staff at school could rob anything of its colour and flavour, given enough time. Often, queueing up at the long counters, we would have to ask the servers what it was we were eating. Sometimes they didn't know themselves. Occasionally, when flummoxed by unidentifiable grey meat nestling next to the khaki cabbage and beige mash, they would confidently assure us that it was roast beef. Despite their misplaced efforts to conjure up visions of Greensleeves and Merrie England, we were not fooled. Nobody went back for seconds. Well, apart from Billy Howells, and he had a tapeworm.

My mother could never understand why, home again at the end of each term, I would fall on her cooking like a wolverine on amphetamine. Despite my mother's tender nutritional ministrations during adolescence, and her ongoing concern at the disparity between food intake and waistline, I continued to surprise her. Being blessed with a high metabolic rate (then not now), I could eat anything I wanted with impunity. Nowadays the tables are turned and I can barely waddle away from the dining table.

At university, there were no rules. Well, with regards to eating at least. I was my own boss. If I wanted to have spaghetti two days running, I would. Or three days even. It didn't matter. My father incidentally holds the family record for consistency when, during his time as a registrar in North Kent, he had veal, ham and egg pie for lunch seventy eight days running. Even the canteen staff were surprised. So he can't talk.

But my real undoing came in my last year at university where, for reasons that are too complicated to explain, I ended up with a room above the Abbey restaurant. The rent included breakfast and an evening meal, taken in the restaurant itself. Fast Eddy did not distinguish between geriatric tourists and priapic students, treating each equally to his theatrically whispered asides on fashion, the economy and modern music. Or whatever went through his head. Eddy saw this running commentary as just an additional benefit for his paying customers. By the end of term, the students knew most of the jokes by heart.

My room overlooked a traffic island where, on winter evenings, a kebab van took up station within easy access of the pubs turning out. Try as I could to resist, the smell of cooking meats and onions wafting through the window nearly always had me scurrying downstairs around eleven o'clock for a large doner with "the works". Strangely, I could always hear my mother saying "Jonathan!"

On summer Sunday evenings, the kebab van's spot was occupied by the Salvation Army who would practice for what seemed like hour upon hour, making my attempts at revision for finals well-nigh impossible. Struggling to get to grips with the Krebs cycle and driven beyond endurance by the third repeat of "What a friend we have in Jesus", I would occasionally pelt them with satsumas.

Food was a lot cheaper when I was at university. Even allowing for the rose tinted spectacles of more than three decades, a ploughman's lunch at the Saracen's Head would set you back no more than a pound. And of course the university refectory was cheaper still being, as he was at pains to tell me, subsidised from my father's taxes. But the cheapest of all was the small canteen in the School of Pharmacy. Run by a tiny Thai woman who could not pronounce 'th', the canteen provided pies, soup, crisps and chocolate.

"I'll have the Cornish pasty and a Mars bar please".

"Turty tree pence prease" she would reply.

Being overgrown kids, we went out of our way to make sure that, whatever we chose for our lunch, it always came to thirty three pence.

"A bowl of soup, a Milky Way and a bag of cheese and onion crisps"

"Turty tree pence prease"

"Chicken pie and a Bakewell slice"

"Turty tree pence prease"

"Sausage roll, bag of chips, cup of tea and a Twix.

"Forty one pence prease"

"What if I don't have the Twix?"

"Turty tree pence prease"

"And at how many revolutions per minute does a standard LP spin?"

"Turty tree and a turd"

I'm sorry. We were young.

## 25 September 2012 – Pong!

One of the most common symptoms of Parkinson's disease is the loss of sense of smell. Often this precedes the stiffness and tremors that lead to diagnosis. After all who would draw a link between the ability to smell perfume and the shakiness of handwriting. Let's face it, it's not an obvious link. And for many newly diagnosed patients, faced with a highly uncertain future of increasing disability, the failure to distinguish between Chanel No 5 and Miss Dior is relatively low on their list of concerns.

But the olfactory pathways are part of the sensory arsenal by which we make sense of the world. Sight, smell, taste, hearing and touch work together to encode every memory we have. Picking up an old postcard can remind you of a happy holiday in Tuscany, hearing a tune on the radio can transport you back to that day you received your A-level results, and feeling the sand between your toes instantly transports you back to your first family holiday, building sand castles with your dad. So it is for smell -- the smell of oil from your bicycle chain, your grandmother's lemon meringue pie, your first girlfriend's perfume. Each sense, in its own way, contributes its own notes to the orchestration of memory.

In Parkinson's, all this is lost. We see well enough, our hearing is unimpaired and our sense of touch is the same (if we can keep still long enough to touch anything). But gradually, sitting unnoticed by our consciousness, our sense of smell glides away. And with it our ability to taste, since smell and taste are two sides of the same coin.

But who could fail to miss the smell of a favourite scent, of new mown grass, of steak and kidney pudding and ripe passionfruit for instance? The gradual erosion of these is among PD's greatest losses, one of its most profound iniquities. And if its loss were instantaneous, nobody would fail to notice. But at first, its departure is unnoticed. Other senses take over. The same happens in darkness where the loss of vision is compensated by an acute increase in one's hearing. And so the sense of smell sidles to the door and departs.

"Haven't those freesias got a beautiful scent?"

"Can you pick up the vanilla and blackcurrants in the wine's bouquet?"

"Surely you can smell the woodsmoke from the pub?"

"The farmer must have let his pigs out, don't you think?"

If the answers to these questions are surprise or bewilderment, then anosmia (the fancy scientific term for loss of smell) has already taken its toll. And suddenly it all makes sense. The fact that food didn't seem to be as tasty as you remembered it, or you find yourself marinating yourself in aftershave and flaring ones nostrils in order to catch the last vestiges of scent.

And even then, the nose plays cruel tricks, confusing the smell of Lynx with dog poo, or overripe pears and biodiesel. And then, even that has gone. The olfactory sound of silence.

There are times when anosmia is actually beneficial. Standing, packed like sardines on the London Underground in August, nose pressed against the armpit of a garlic loving Abyssinian weightlifter, most would give their right arms for anosmia. Or when the putrid wind from the sewage farm is blowing hard enough to fade the curtains and make eyes water, three cheers for anosmia.

Since food has little taste these days, I find myself eating foods I formerly rejected and resented. Peas taste like beans, apples like pears and Weetabix like cardboard (no change there then).

And finally, after fifty four years, I find that my mother was right all along about unfamiliar meat. Guinea fowl, whale blubber, shark's fin – it matters not because it certainly does, as she would say, taste like chicken.

### 30 September 2012 – Two Americans

Two Americans have, in very different ways, unwittingly taught me two important life lessons. No, but I follow your reasoning, I am not talking about Laurel and Hardy. Nor Abbott and Costello. No, the gentlemen in question were Mark Twain and Thomas Jonathan Jackson. Although the latter may be new to you, you will almost certainly have heard of Twain.

More than any other author perhaps, Mark Twain is responsible for introducing British adolescents to American literature through the chronicled adventures of Tom Sawyer and the exuberantly named Huckleberry Finn. Viewed by many, Faulkner and Hemingway included, as the father of the American novel, Twain's output amounts to some thirteen novels and other sundries. Hemingway even went so far as to say that *"All modern American literature comes from one book by Mark Twain called 'Huckleberry Finn.' There was nothing before. There has been nothing as good since"*. Strong praise indeed.

Twain was inevitably a rich source of quotations from the humorous to the inspirational but none resonates more deeply with me than this:

*"The two most important days in your life are the day you are born and the day you find out why"*.

And in those twenty one words are distilled a potent idea and a gnawing certainty - the idea that life should have purpose and that, sooner or later, through circumstance or happenstance, that purpose will be made clear.

A good friend of mine from Texas, diagnosed with Parkinson's five years ago, found a form of salvation. After the usual feelings of depression, he emerged, with urgency and drive, into a world of advocacy. In a strange way, and one he would not have chosen, Parkinson's had given him his purpose.

And so it has for me. Like many others before, and doubtless many more after, I am a soldier in this war on Parkinson's. And, if it is to be won, it is a war that must be fought on many fronts. By the best research, by improvements in patient health, by public education, and by changing the political will. These are bold ambitions and will not be achieved by a single individual.

In this war we contribute in our own way, in the way we feel most comfortable. For some that is very public, marching with placards, signing petitions, rabble-rousing militancy. For others it will be behind desks, lobbying politicians or educating the public. In any war, the control of information is paramount. This is no different. And for some, the battlefront is in the world's laboratories and research institutes, in white coats, conducting the research that will ultimately defeat Parkinson's. And then there are those others, myself included, who use websites to make sure that our victories are publicised, that the soldiers are equipped and deployed where they are in the best position to use their talents against the enemy - and to know where the breaches in the line will come and to send reinforcements. The tactics of battle. Which brings me to my second American.

The second man, Thomas Jonathan Jackson, was a Confederate general during the American civil war. My father, at the time I was born, was fascinated by the American civil war and, although he has never said as much, I am convinced that I was named after his favourite general. Jackson was a master tactician, using the limited resources at his disposal to wreak havoc for the enemy. During the famous Valley campaign, Jackson moved his small army (a mere seventeen thousand strong) more than six hundred miles in a month and a half against a force that numbered sixty thousand, inflicting five significant defeats on the union Army. Jackson had a way of making limited resources go further. An inspirational leader and tactical genius, Jackson's command of the Stonewall Brigade probably extended the Civil War by a couple of years as the South briefly entertained the fanciful possibility of victory. His death in 1863 at the Battle of Chancellorsville effectively ended the last vestiges of hope.

Despite his tactical mastery, it was Jackson's courage, and that of his troops, at the first battle of Manassas, standing firm in the face of a heavy Union assault, that earned him the nickname by which he is most commonly known. "Stonewall" Jackson.

Jackson acknowledged throughout his life that his army was never as strong as needed. But he never complained, and used his tactical brilliance with the limited resources at his disposal to wage war on his enemy. He believed that the best form of defence was attack and his ability to strike fast and hard at the enemy won many a battle against overwhelming odds.

Two men with very different ideas. Twain the inspirational thinker and Jackson the decisive doer. Between them they have taught me that this battle, this war even, will be won by brilliant ideas efficiently executed. They have taught me that it is vital to think in depth and equally essential to act swiftly, decisively and with purpose. I am no Twain or Stonewall but I recognize in them the qualities I must try to bring to the fight. I see the ground on which I will stand and fight.

I can't speak for other chronic illnesses with any authority, and it's probably wrong to generalise, but there seems to me to be a special bond among people with Parkinson's. In many ways this is surprising, especially so when you consider how heterogeneous a bunch we are. Some freeze, some shake, some stumble, some mumble. My Parkinson's is not your Parkinson's. I may quiver and shake while you may be a frozen statue. It's hard to believe that so different a group of symptoms can still be part of the same illness. But despite these variations on the theme, we recognise each other as soldiers in the same army.

We are fighting a war on Parkinson's and, though it may often feel different at the battlefront, as our comrades fall around us, it is a war our enemy cannot win. We will slow our retreat. We will draw a line and we will stand and fight, shoulder to shoulder. Scientist, physician and patient will link arms and say "Enough". We will stand like a stone wall against our enemy. We owe it to all the fallen.

We will hold the line.

And when we have won and lie exhausted on the field of battle, in the last words spoken by Stonewall, "Let us cross the river and rest under the shade of the trees".

Printed in Great Britain
by Amazon.co.uk, Ltd.,
Marston Gate.